Furs, Feathers, Frogs

What I Learned
from the Animals
in My World

FURS,
FEATHERS,
FROGS

What I Learned
from the Animals
in My World

DIANNE CORFIELD SEARLE MACDONALD

Published by Searle Publishing,
Auburn, Washington.

All book photographs courtesy of the Macdonald family.
All part title page artwork by Dianne Macdonald.
Cover and author photos by Richard Breitenbach.
Cover and interior design by Mi Ae Lipe (whatnowdesign.com).

Printed in the United States of America.

To contact the author or order additional copies:
Dianne Macdonald
diannemacdonaldauthor@gmail.com

First Edition, 2025
Print book ISBN: 979-8-218-57494-9
Ebook ISBN: 979-8-218-57495-6
Library of Congress Control Number: 2025900095

Dedicated to Chuck and Laurie,
the two wonderful children I sprouted,
and to all the critters who barked, meowed, neighed,
ribbited, flew, hopped, and crawled through my world
as I learned to more fully appreciate
and enjoy all of God's wonderful world of nature.

CONTENTS

Introduction   ix

PART I | TAKING CHANCES

A Feathered Prologue   3

  1   I Should Have Known Better   6
  2   Prelude to the Crapshoot   11
  3   Luck of the Draw   16
  4   Encounter at the Cathouse   20
  5   Still Hitting Zero   24
  6   Breaking Even   27
  7   A Pair of Aces to Keep   31
  8   Waiting for the Hurricane   35
  9   Forty-Seven Degrees Below?   40
10   Spill-My-Guts Time   43
11   Snow Times Three   49
12   A Disturbing Interlude   53
13   Added Bonuses   55
14   Heading Home   59
15   Getting Home   63
16   Seattle Interim   67
17   Our Sky Fell In   71
18   Litter Letter from Gran   74
19   Other Pains   78
20   Different Happenings   82
21   The Hero Who Saved the Day   88
22   Produce, Hutches, and Coops   92
23   Looking over My Shoulder While Walking Ahead   96

PART II | ASKING QUESTIONS

A Frog Prologue   101

24 Cages, Tanks, and Plants   105
25 Into Everyone's Heart   109
26 A Pair of Calicoes   116
27 Frustrations: Flivers, Fleas, and Fireplaces   121
28 Mr. T Saved My Day   126
29 Voice of Spring   130
30 A Fowl Week   134
31 I Can Coexist—Yes, I Can, Except…   139
32 No Redeeming Love: Flies, Slugs, Moles   145
33 Three Stooges: Straight, Kinked, and Knotted   149
34 No Redeeming Love: Mice and Opossums   154
35 Moral Dilemma: Who Is the Scorekeeper?   158
36 Through the Telescope of Time   162
37 A Log of Barking   165
38 If One Is Good, Are Two Better?   171
39 Looking Ahead, Walking into the Next Century   179

PART III | SHIFTING OUTLOOKS

Fur Kids Prologue   185

40 Senior-Style Musical Chairs   188
41 Fur Kids' Trek South   193
42 Down and Ousted   196
43 Silly Adds Texture to My Life   201
44 Fur Kids Amalgamation   207
45 Play Nice Now   211
46 Feline Potty Training   215
47 Intruders from All Directions   219
48 Too Painful a Decision   223
49 Lines to Draw   228
50 Still More Miles   233

Epilogue   239
Acknowledgments   241
About the Author   242

INTRODUCTION

The source of Dianne's best entertainment was not Broadway or travel—it was the animals inside her home and those outside on her land. While her children were growing up, there was a white rat up the sleeve of a little boy riding his bike, eighty-five baby guppies born in a little girl's bedroom fish tank, a box turtle rescued from a road in Virginia, and a bat kidnapped from Eastern Washington to relocate in their magnolia tree. For a few years, a donkey's bray served as a doorbell. Cats and dogs gave birth to second-generation pets, some of whom stayed for a week and others for twenty years, bringing love, companionship, and fun.

Each had a story. Each touched hearts with tears of joy and tears of sorrow. Each brought glorious and fun memories as well as painful and tragic ones. The parade of pets cycling through the stages of their lives brought about choices and decisions, and, as with everything in life, each gave a lesson to be learned, which, in the process, hopefully led to new growth.

Past the impetuousness of her younger days, Dianne applied deeper thought and began to question choices while more animals cycled in and she dealt with overflowing fish tanks, fleas, and excess dog fur. While gardening, landscaping, and clearing her home's two acres in Auburn, Washington, she spent more time outside observing ducks, frogs, squirrels, rabbits, woodpeckers, and a coyote. She also impulsively killed an opossum in her woodpile and found new levels of frustration over ants, moles, yellow jackets, more opossums, and the neighbor's dogs.

Adding reflection to former decisions, she raised moral questions: What *is* the right thing to do? Whose world *is* this anyway? *Who* gets to do the deciding? And where *do* you draw the line?" In questioning her impulsive actions through her early years, for the first time she considered how those choices affected others and her children's lives: *Early decisions determine so much of the rest of our lives.* What were the results of her lack of thought? What actions bring the greatest good with the least intrusion to animals and environment? And to children?

PART I

TAKING CHANCES

A Feathered Prologue

*W*ings whirred, feathers flew, and the air filled with quacking and flapping. Jolted out of my reverie, my hands full of weeds, I looked up. Two feet in front of me, a mama duck from my pond was making a terrible fuss. She rushed at me in a valiant attempt to distract me from the object of her distress. Behind her quivered a fuzz-covered creature with a head too large for its plump little body. I realized that Mama was trying to threaten me away from her little one. Then she turned to it and scolded. I think I heard her say, "You get back home where you belong, and do it right now. Don't be wasting any time about it, either. Move!" She may have even added, "And just you wait, you'll hear from your father, too." She started herding her feathered kid back in the direction of the pond.

First, I thought, *How did they happen to be up here next to the driveway? Did the baby go by itself and Mama came to find it? Or did she actually hatch it here? Maybe she just took it for a nice little stroll today to see the world.* In fifty years, I had never seen baby ducks more than twenty feet away from the pond, and this was further than seventy yards.

This year's ducklings hatched out a short while ago. I had not even seen them out of the water. This must be one precocious kid. Mama shooed her baby toward home with a tirade of dire threats to never run away again. As I stood and watched them flustering along the edge of the driveway, they stamped over the *Ajuga* and swished through the elephant ear plants, passing a frog who leaped onto a rock to get out of the way. Instead of following the ditch line along the edge of the pasture to return to the pond, they came through a walkway into the yard.

I worried they would not make it home without being found by my furred pets, so I followed them to influence the direction of their journey, or at least to guard them from my predator cats who might get that baby if given a chance. And then I thought, *Where is Sitka?* Three or four years ago while washing dishes, I had looked out the window and saw a sight that sent me screaming from the house. My husky was coming from the ditch on the other side of the pasture with a duckling in her mouth. At my ruckus, Sitka dropped the baby, looking at me with a guilty "Uh-oh, caught in the act" look. The duckling, evidently unhurt, immediately scrambled to the ditch and swam back into the pond.

Now, I saw my current canine standing at the front corner of the house watching the feathered parade with a drop of saliva rolling from her part-husky, part-wolf tongue. I hurried to run interference.

Mama was still squawking and cackling, hurling admonitions at her toddler to get going faster. All the while she flapped her wings and was probably adding, "And don't you *ever* leave again without my permission. Next time you listen to what you are told."

I tried to head them onto a pathway back to the pasture and away from three fur kids of the feline variety who were watching from the back of the deck. Instead of finding the break in the wire fence, the ducks kept on this side of it and trampled through the vegetable garden. They wove around cabbage plants, stomped over beet greens, and squished green onions before racing under the blueberry bushes to come to the end of the fence. Reaching familiar territory, they tore across the remaining pasture to the pond. I heard a soft murmur of "Ah, safety!" as they splashed off from the shore. That little guy was going to have a fun tale to tell his brothers and sisters. I could hear him now: "You should have been there. It was so fun. I ran away from home ... and ... I almost made it."

Excitement over, with ducks and ducklings peacefully swimming in the pond, I turned back to my weeding and caught sight of a squirrel running along a maple branch. As he scampered, the horizontal branch became smaller and smaller, but he kept going. I stopped to see what he would do, then gasped when he jumped and nimbly landed on a small branch of a neighboring maple. I thought, *Good going, little fellow.* Several crows swept by on their route to the neighbor's porch on the other side of our house. I knew where they were headed. The window at my computer desk looks out on their porch, and when I write, I see their five dogs eating breakfast. Then I see the crows swooping in to enjoy the leftovers. Later I deal with the new deluge of weeds they have gifted me from the seeds in their poop.

I looked back to see the baby ducklings follow Mama to the other end of the pond. Depending on the rains of the year, the pond starts filling sometime between October and December and the ducks return. At first, as many as twenty arrive, and then three or four pairs stay to mate and raise their young. My first act every morning is to look out, count the pairs of ducks, and in the spring, watch for the first appearance of their little downy creatures. Last fall, the pond filled and the ducks returned on Election Day. Their return gives a promise of hope that spring will follow a hard winter, and, like the election, a look ahead to a new beginning filled with high expectations.

Ah, new beginnings. What exuberance the young have. How innocent they are. The whole world is ahead of them, and all seems possible with every day spent looking forward to something new. No thought is given to the difficulties of tomorrow. Maybe the night absorbs the worries and the problems of the young so that each dawn can bring forth a fresh start.

I thought of the duckling today, of his journey, and the impetuousness of youth. Like him, I struck out on my own early in life, doing what I wanted, not listening to the lessons I was given, and without thinking of later consequences. Oh, the innocence of the duckling. Yes, and of myself back in those early days when animals started cycling through my life. Sixty-plus years ago, I started a family. Fifty-plus years ago, I bought my house and two acres. In between, I set out on an adventure with no idea of what was ahead of me or what the future would bring.

And the duckling? What lies ahead for him? What further experiences will he have? Will he learn the needed lessons to avert future disasters?

Neither the duckling nor I were given a telescope to see the consequences of what would come in later years, no periscope to peer around the corners of our decisions, no binoculars to bring choices into sharper focus. No, we did not know from the beginning how things would turn out. The duckling will just have to live it out, as I did. Yes, one adventure at a time.

1

I Should Have Known Better

*Y*ears ago, I disregarded the admonitions of others, made a major life choice without thought for the future, and set out on my own adventure. It was one of those hormonal happenings, a situation to inspire a later "Oh, yeah, I should have known better."

On a March morning in 1964, with too much to do, too little time, and tired and weary, I was late starting out. It was a clear day, and after gassing up in Fife with a mileage of 64,140 on my 1958 Plymouth wagon, I set out to situate my children with my folks for two weeks as I prepared to run away from home. I met Nick at the appointed place, where we hooked an already loaded U-Haul trailer onto his truck and set out on a 3,065-mile trek across the United States to settle in the tideflats of Virginia. My mother-in-law would fly Chuck, my six-year-old son, and Laurie, my five-year-old daughter, to us when we found a house.

Nick was heart-weary. He was leaving his two small children behind. For me, it was good to have decision-making over, to be done with planning and packing, and to not think about the good job, friends, relatives, ten acres, and piano I was leaving behind. My cat, Nikolai, took a turn on the seat beside me, flicked his tail a couple of times, and fell asleep. No time for second-guessing now, just driving.

Before too many miles passed, I was deep into a reverie of the events leading up to this moment. It happens without fail—every time I drive long distances, I start mulling over my life. I had graduated from college at the half-year mark in 1961 with high honors, a home economics major, an art minor, and a teaching certificate for grades one through twelve. I had two beautiful, delightful children and a divorce from their sperm donor—that term used for a father who never parented. I had never really had a marriage as such. Too immature to make wise choices, I had married my first boyfriend from high school. He

6

was even more immature and could not think of handling the responsibilities of settling down to marriage or fatherhood. We separated both times I was pregnant, and the second time I did not welcome him back. I had moved in with my folks, enrolled in college to finish the remaining two and a half years, and begun to support my children and me.

Fresh out of college and forced into the world, I started feeling it might be an all-right place to be. A fellow teacher at that first job had remarked, "You have the world by the tail on a downhill pull." This tall, knowledgeable, talkative Norwegian immediately began to pursue me. Having barely dated in high school and focused on college and children with no social life for three years, I was quite taken by his attention. I held off on becoming serious with him until the next school year, but once I settled into a new home and job, I succumbed.

Besides being a history teacher, Nick was in the Coast Guard Reserve on active duty during the summers. In 1964 he decided to quit his teaching job and was assigned to a Coast Guard station in Virginia. He would be leaving in March, and he asked me to go with him, saying we would be married there. Might I have known better?

With this prospect, I needed to quit my job in Tacoma and not only leave the house my children and I were living in and pack our household belongings in a U-Haul trailer to transport across the country, but also let a house and ten acres from my divorce go back to the bank. The children would be uprooted from school—Chuck in the first grade and Laurie in kindergarten—and leaving both sets of grandparents. Not mature enough to tell my folks forthrightly that I was going across the country with a man, and rather than risk their wrath, I told them I would be going to school. Mother was convinced I would not survive driving cross-country in the middle of winter and that my children would not only have no father but no mother as well. My stubbornness has won out through a lot of my life. It did once more, and I struck out on my adventure. Oh yes, I should have known better.

My reminiscing was over when we stopped in Pendleton for dinner, wrote postcards home, and took our road-weary bodies to bed. We awoke at 3 in the morning to … the fragrance of cat. Nick couldn't find where Nikolai had peed until he put on his trousers. The cat was the only one unpopular until my sense of humor got the best of me; I laughed and became unpopular also. Nick, a cat person, had named our cat Nikolai Rimsky-Korsakov, and he did not remain unhappy for long. After I fed Nikolai and got him settled back in the car, Nick adjusted the light wires to the trailer, and then we were on our way through rolling, light-gold wheat stubble set off against darkly burned areas and brown earth. Those are the warm and subtle colors I love—good for my troubled mind.

In drab, cold Rupert, Idaho, the motel's shower water reeked of sulfur, which left my hair not only straight but also stinking. By this time, Nick and I were already both unhappy and questioning our decisions. Nikolai also must have questioned our choices, because in the morning he escaped his leash. We spent two hours searching and calling for him before finally deciding to leave without him. We hoped he would find a very good family to take him in—maybe one whose money lasted to the end of the month. Whenever I ran out of money, I had fed Nikolai people food; he'd show his displeasure at our leftovers by lifting his tail to spray in the house.

We drove on with heavy hearts indeed. I kicked myself for trying to bring him along. After filling the gas tank with eleven gallons priced at thirty-seven cents a gallon for a total of four dollars and eleven cents, we were on our way. Many hours later, when I passed an aromatic silage truck, my car started to swerve uncontrollably. I slowed down and pulled to the side of the road with a flat tire. Nick's truck with my U-Haul trailer was way ahead, but I was grateful to see he had been paying attention and stopped also. I flagged down a truck and asked the driver if he would please tell the owner of the truck and trailer ahead that I had a flat tire. When I admonished the driver to then stand back and close his ears, he grinned from ear to ear.

Nick came back to the car and upon seeing the situation, remarked, "Well, I suppose we have to change it." Little did he know what was yet to come, for at that moment I realized the ramifications of my method of packing. In the last-minute rush to get everything done and wanting to include all the children's belongings while the available room was filling up rapidly, I made some foolish choices. Oh, silly me, I had never considered the possibility of a flat tire on the trip. Nor had I thought of the configuration of my station wagon, with its location of the spare tire and jack. I pride myself on my efficient organizing, and I used every nook and cranny, including the awkward space between the back doors and the rear seats. Into that space I had dumped all the small toy parts and pieces from boxes that would not fit anywhere else. It was under this area that the jack rested.

Nick blithely opened the back of the wagon and pulled out several big boxes of kitchen, household, and clothing effects. He was able to get down to the floor and retrieve the tire. "Now I need a jack—I suppose it's under the rest of that stuff?"

"Ahhhh, yeesss it is, but can't we use your jack?"

His response was immediate: "No, we can't; it won't fit."

"Oh, *no*." Yuk. In the face of male disgust, anger, and frustration, I removed clothes from the back of the wagon and put them in his truck, trying to avoid the gas and oil cans. I placed a basket with jewelry spilling from it onto the side of the road, adding to it a box of art, sewing, and bookkeeping supplies. I lifted the seat, only to find that I had cleared the wrong side. As I wailed, "Oh no, it's on the other side," Nick started to open that door.

"No! Stop, you can't open that door!" I cried.

Exasperated, he asked, "Why not?"

"Because the kid's blocks are down there."

"Why didn't you put them in a box?"

"Because there was empty space where a box wouldn't fit."

"Well, we have to open it!" Matter-of-factly, he flung the door open. Of course, that door faced the roadside, and all the blocks, toy parts, and pieces fell out on the road. He then moved another toy box, a box of decorations, a phonograph, and a sewing machine. Lifting the seat, he retrieved the jack.

Finally glad to be getting on with a straightforward job familiar to him, he proceeded to change the tire. Meanwhile, I picked up all the blocks and toy parts, putting them in a basket. I was glad I am not a crying person; I really felt like doing just that. After I rearranged the toy box, the decorations box, our little TV, phonograph, and sewing machine, I shut the side door. I placed the big kitchen box back where it belonged and shut the back of the car. On the other side, I put back the art box and basket and shut that door, filling in the space.

A patrolman passing by stopped, tilted his head to the side, raised an eyebrow, and asked, "What is going on?" This came across to me, of course, as "What are you dumb yokels doing?" I shoved stuff that had been dumped into the front seat over into the back, organized my journal and map to use as we continued our travels, and signaled I was ready to be on the road again. Soon I was back to following the sign on the back of the rented U-Haul trailer, which proclaimed "Nationwide Rents It." I was already fed up looking at it. So many hours had been spent with measuring tape and graph paper while I plotted the arrangement for our furniture and belongings to fit as much in as possible and deciding which possessions to leave behind. After two days of looking at that sign, I would have liked to rip it off, and there were still five more to go. My humor gradually returned with the hopeful thought, *It is packed better now than it was before, and we are ready for the next flat tire.*

I realized how difficult it would have been to go through all those gyrations of changing the tire if Nikolai were still with us, but I missed him terribly as we drove on without mishap for the rest of the trip. I did not know then that on my return trip, two years later in the same Plymouth wagon, I would make it safely back to Washington State with two children, a poodle pup named Kookla, and a cat named Sasha—all safely intact. Nikolai, fondly remembered, was the first of an even dozen cats to enter my life and then leave in one way or another. Some were short-timers while others lived nearly twenty years with us. A couple of them were heartbreakers but all were heartwarmers, as were the other animals that were to join our lives.

2

PRELUDE TO THE CRAPSHOOT

*E*very geographical area seems to have its own advantages and dis-advantages of weather, animals, and insects. I had left the Pacific Coast weather of several nice days, a few halfhearted snow days, one or two thunderstorms, a periodic flood, and many gray, plain days of drizzle. Traveling in March through bright, strong sunshine in eastern Washington; wet, slushy snow in Oregon; blinding blizzards through Idaho; and thick, glassy ice layered with snow in Wyoming and Nebraska, we were met in Ohio with the energetic blowing of Ole Thor accompanied by dramatic thunder and lightning storms. Through Pennsylvania, all the water faucets in heaven opened wide; I found nature has strong water pressure on the East Coast.

Upon our arrival in Virginia in early spring, the days were rather colorless and ordinary. There was a period of snow—not an immense amount, but enough for the children to build a real snowman for the first time, instead of putting snowballs in the freezer as they did in Tacoma. Later, the weather turned to summer, with beautiful sunny days of eighty degrees and several unpleasant ones in the nineties. When the thermometer soared over one hundred, being a middle-range person, I took to bed. Thankfully, I raised independent children, and social services were not called in. My kids built tents and forts, and Chuck slept outside in a hammock.

Not far from our house was a road that wound along a reservoir. That is where we were first exposed to the animals in this new environment. I could not believe the number of wild critters lying deceased on the side of the road—and in the middle of it. The people in the South speak slower than those in more northern climes. Maybe the warmer climate also encourages more sluggish road-crossing than in our cooler Pacific Northwest. Turtles wandered onto the road too slowly to make it safely across. A six- to nine-inch box turtle seemed monstrous to us compared to the little two- or three-inch kind we had seen in pet stores.

Of course, it didn't take long for Chuck to convince me to stop the car so he could capture one of those fascinating creatures. It had intricate yellow designs on its dark greenish-brown shell, with the same pattern repeated on its legs and head. When we looked the turtle in the eye, he blinked, blinked again, pulled his head back, and closed the door to his portable home. His message was unmistakably, "Thank you kindly, but I'd like to be alone now."

Undeterred, Chuck gathered three of these turtles that were wandering up from the marsh behind us. They did not stay around long, but they were fun to watch while they were there. He asked if we could take one back to the Pacific Northwest with us when we went. "We could make a cage for it."

Laurie said, "Remember the turtle at Auntie Joan's house that laid an egg in front of the Christmas tree? It didn't want to be left out of the gift giving."

We both laughed and replied, "Oh, yeah."

By means of roadkill, I was introduced to another new and very strange animal. It had black and white fur on its rather rounded body, a white face, and a very long pink nose. Those with mouths open at the time of their demise revealed angry-looking teeth. There was a hairless tail equaling the length of this creature's body. I thought them to be extremely ugly. I soon learned they were opossums. Little did I know that twenty years later, I would run across two of them on my own land in the Pacific Northwest.

On the East Coast, what the locals call mountains, I call hills. Whatever the label, they are much lower and not rocky like those in the Pacific Northwest. The rivers are not rapid but wider and slower with seawater flowing up into them. We lived on a section that was rather like a cul-de-sac with houses on our side of the street backed onto the marshland. This gave us a green, private backyard and Chuck and the neighbor boys a prime opportunity to catch crabs. Periodically, a group of them would announce a crabbing expedition. Finding pail and string or fishline, they went to different houses looking for smelly herring or old bacon. Then they'd put a nail through the bait so it would sink,

Arrival in Virginia.

and they'd go down to the tidewater to catch wiggly-squiggly crabs. Sometimes one of the crabs lost its way and scuttled up into the yard. Of course, this was always good for a few moments of commotion as Laurie and her friends jumped around squealing. Later, to my horror, I learned that the water also contained water moccasins.

Most of the mothers didn't want to be bothered cooking crabs. The children soon found out I liked crab and didn't mind cooking them. So, they brought them to my back door. "Mrs. Searle, would you like some crab?" And then an eager plea: "If you are going to cook them, can we watch?" What they wanted was to see them go into the boiling water and turn orange. I was glad to add them to my list of food-gathering experiences. I missed the trout fishing and yearly clam digging of my childhood in the Pacific Northwest, as well as the frequent oyster gathering in Gig Harbor.

In Virginia, every house had a child, each child had a dog, and, of course, each dog had its own society of ticks and fleas. A teenager named Artie lived next door with his shaggy collie named Cookie, who came to visit often. The children would pick the ticks off her, throw these blood-filled critters onto the carport floor, and then squish them with their bikes. One section of the carport was covered with blood splatters.

I do not know when flea and tick treatments became prevalent, but either the neighbors thought the infestations were not important enough to be bothered with, or they did not want to use chemicals on their pets, or thought the bugs were *so* prolific that no product would remedy the situation. In any case, the children rescued Cookie from this affliction. When the kids played in the woods or the marsh, they returned with ticks also. These hangers-on seemed not only harmless but also painless. In fact, the kids enjoyed their new sport of picking ticks off each other before the evening bath.

When I think about the animals in my life, I realize how few were in my life as a child compared to the ongoing zoo my children were to experience growing up. While I was young, my father had a mutt named Punk who was not allowed in the house. On a rare occasion, Daddy was known to sneak Punk inside, but only when Mother was gone for the evening. Mother had grown up on a farm and seemed to view animals as functional (such as farm cats for hunting rodents and dogs for herding livestock and guarding against intruders), but not as pets for fun and love. Also, fur definitely did not belong in her clean and tidy house.

During the time I was in the third to sixth grades, we had a white cat named Nikki. She was grand enough to sport one gray eye and one green eye that would turn blue at times, but she was not grand enough to be allowed inside. In the summer after graduation from high school, I inadvertently played a dirty trick on my mother, perchance getting even for the lack of animal love in my childhood. I came home with an adorable kitten, with no thought that in a few weeks, I would wave good-bye to family and kitten as I went off to college; the kitten was bequeathed to my younger brother.

Like so many people disagreeing with something from their child-hood who vowed to do differently themselves, I was determined: "*I* will have animals in *my* house." Because of this, I looked ahead to permitting my children to get close to pets; dogs and cats would squirm around the edges of board games on the floor, wriggle their heads into laps during story time, and snuggle under the bedcovers at night. The only pets I would keep outside at my house would be the horses, donkey, and rabbits. The nonpets would be kept outside also—the yellow jackets, moles, slugs, ants, coyotes, raccoons, opossums, and, of course, the ducks and frogs. But those would come later.

I promised Chuck a dog and Laurie a cat once we got settled in Virginia, and it was here, close to the mouth of the York River on Chesapeake Bay, that we started our encounters with pets of all sorts. This endeavor brought questions I had not considered: How and where will we get a pet? Will it be healthy? Will it fit in with our family? Will it be fun and like us? Will we like it? And, of great importance to the mother—me—will it be trainable? And ... how soon? These ideas floated around the periphery of my consciousness while we settled in and became acquainted with our surroundings.

I would soon learn that when choosing an animal, you just have to take what comes. You can never know what will develop in the way of temperament, health, or interactions, nor do you know what will happen in terms of accidental happenings. The vagaries of life can step in at any time with incidents or situations never anticipated. With animals, like cards and relationships, you must know when to hold, when to fold, and if you should walk away, or perchance, maybe even run. It is always a venture marked by uncertainty, as we would soon find out—an animal crapshoot.

3

LUCK OF THE DRAW

*M*y number-one animal mistake was taking Nikolai in the car across the country. My number-two mistake evolved from a promise to Chuck of a dog for his birthday. Across the street was a spaniel variety named Pepper, while his next-door neighbor of terrier origin was named Toby. Behind him was Queenie, the progenitor of our first puppy I accepted for free. He was a cute little creature immediately adored by one small seven-year-old boy. Little did I know then of the problems and expenses to follow.

This pup did not take easily to training, and I soon deduced he did not live up to his name either—Sparky. We noticed a lack of hair, pinkness of stomach, and sores on his legs, leading to the first of many trips down the road to a friendly vet who probably outfitted his wife for a year on the money we were to dole out to him. He informed us that the prevailing condition was a fungus infection; he treated Sparky and sent us home. Sparky appeared to get better, the sores became less obvious, and Chuck started smiling again. Soon the condition returned. Back to the vet we went, a discouraged Chuck holding his little puppy tightly to his chest, both of them with big, sad brown eyes. Again, we returned home with a treated dog and hope in our hearts.

After several trips back and forth with improvement returning to a worsened condition, the vet said, "Sparky has mange, and it will probably last months." We treated the situation ourselves according to the vet's instructions. He added, "It is often associated with hormones at puberty, most commonly starting at around four months, and was probably genetic, with others in the litter affected." With this deal of the cards, I was having a hard time knowing whether to hold or to fold.

Finally, we packed up the dog and toddled down the road for the opinion of another vet, telling him of the time, worry, hurt, and money already spent. He examined Sparky and informed us that

The children with their ill-fated first pets:
Laurie holding her deformed kitten and Chuck with the mangy Sparky.

some mange, if it is in the glands and bloodstream, cannot be cured. He added, "Since there's been no improvement with all the care you have given him, most likely that's the case here. When there is a severe immune-system deficiency, the pet will commonly have secondary bacterial infections, and although it will respond for a short period of time, it will prove to be incurable." He added it is often associated with hormones at puberty, most commonly starting at around four months, and was probably genetic with others in the litter affected. So, a little boy with wide, moist brown eyes, clutching a wiggly little part-beagle, agreed to leave his dog with the vet, who knew more about it than we did and could take better care of him.

Oh, what a mother. I don't even remember telling my children about Santa Claus, and now this fabrication! Of course, it is always easier for the parent when giving such an excuse to a child. I thought the realization of what was to actually happen to his dog could wait for a less intense moment. The loss to my little fellow, who had welcomed his very own pet with the huge and open heart he's always been known for, was already so great. Chuck would have no more jumpy, warm greetings at his return from school, no more bundle of energy screeching down the hall, and no longer a squirmy, cuddly bedfellow.

The decision for the dog's fate didn't have to be second-guessed; it was for the best. He really was miserable; we had tried our best for a cure to make him better, and we found that impossible. It was better for Chuck because a sick dog that wasn't *sparky*, even with the encouragement of the name, was certainly not the same as a healthy dog. And it was better for the neighborhood as our dog could infect other dogs around him.

A little sidelight about Sparky's siblings came to the fore at about this time. Two other puppies from the same litter also had mange. They were so emaciated that I felt ill looking at them. I asked their owners to keep them at home, telling them, "They are sick and need to be taken care of. They can infect other dogs." When they brought them around the third time, I called the humane society, and shortly afterward, the children said the dogs were gone.

With that, our first very disappointing animal experience in Virginia ended. I was glad we held out as long as we did. We had tried our best with Sparky, but when it was time, we cut loose and walked away. However, years later, I would rethink and question that choice, as with several others.

We did have a winning-hand interlude that was delightful. While Sparky was still with us, the people next door planned to go away for several days and asked us to keep an eye on their cat. Tiger, a big fluffy white feline, hung out around our house and the children and our pup enjoyed playing with her. At first, I questioned the choice of name since she was such a gentle soul. When I examined her face further, I realized how very tigerlike her features were. At this time, however, what was most noticeable was how very pregnant her belly was.

One evening, the children let Tiger into the house, and we enjoyed watching her and our pup play. I began to notice the cat was behaving strangely; she stopped what she was doing and shuddered. I didn't need to be an obstetrician to realize what might happen that night, and I thought, "Oh, I want us to be a part of this. It would be such a wonderful experience if she would pop, right here, with us watching."

I felt I should call Joyce, the neighbor's daughter, who lived across the creek. Joyce's daughter was the same age as Laurie, and I thought she should be given the chance to spectate this wondrous event. But I so wanted us to see this birth that I rationalized, "I don't *really* know what is happening, and I don't *really* want to bother Joyce unnecessarily this late at night." Needless to say, I selfishly neglected to make the call.

Instead, we got a box and a clean towel and settled the soon-to-be-new mommy in the box on the couch. Three very excited people waited, hopping around, exclaiming, and bursting with anticipation. Soon three pairs of wide eyes watched three darling little wet pink kittens emerge into this big wide world. What an experience—we were so thrilled. After the second birth, I called Joyce and found out she wanted no part of this procedure anyway. She wanted to wait until it was all over to pick them up the next day. This assuaged my guilt over keeping the whole process to ourselves.

When Joyce came the next day to pick up the cat with her new little kittens, we told her we would love to have one of the babies for Laurie's birthday in June. By then, they would be old enough to separate from Tiger. We had lost Nikolai; Chuck had had a puppy; and Laurie wanted a kitten. Of course, it would be fun to have a cat we had *delivered*. I thought it was a done deal, and it didn't occur to me to ask the Collins when they returned. Later we found out they had given all the kittens away and had Tiger fixed. We were very disappointed at that deal of the cards. And we should have learned then the valuable lesson of clarifying exactly what we wanted! And then stopping and verifying that it was understood!

Oh well, a valuable lesson for another day.

4

ENCOUNTER AT THE CATHOUSE

That first summer, quite by accident, my children and I had one of those special times to be fondly remembered even fifty years later. Visiting Washington, DC, we happened to drive by the Smithsonian National Zoological Park and swung around to go in. I was so glad we did.

Walking across the zoo grounds, we saw at least one hundred men, women, and children spread out over a large area. It was either a community gathering or one very large family picnic. All the women were dressed alike in turquoise cotton bonnets and long dresses reaching to their high-top black shoes. The men looked very solemn in black stove-top hats and black suits with shirts of the same fabric and color as the women's dresses. All the children, regardless of their size, wore outfits identical to their elders, as if instead of being regarded as children, they were merely miniature adults. I wished later I had been brave enough—or maybe intrusive enough—to stop and ask questions. But I didn't.

I read a sign that this zoo was not solely for the purpose of entertainment, but also for biological research. As part of the Smithsonian Institution, its first animals were those that taxidermists had used as models. It was started in 1889, and by 1964, its approximately three thousand animals resided on 163 acres in Rock Creek Park, about fifteen minutes from downtown Washington, DC.

One of the reasons for establishing the zoo was to preserve the American bison, and we saw those huge creatures. We also saw a much smaller African buffalo. The giraffe weighed two tons, averaged fourteen to sixteen feet with a nineteen-foot maximum, and sported spots in the shape of leaves. The power of suggestion weighs heavy with me, and when I see those stately creatures, the thought of holding up one of those necks does also.

There were several animals I had never seen before. From Liberia was a mother pygmy hippopotamus with her baby. Their very smooth, shiny skin was weird-looking, as were their two-sectioned feet. We saw regular hippopotamuses (or maybe it's hippopotamice). We learned they are more akin to the pig family, even if their name means *river horse*. They have a very reddish tinge, especially around the neck and head. We also saw rhinoceros with huge horns; these animals weren't so small themselves.

The armadillo was sleeping, so we couldn't see him very well, although his shell looked much softer than I would have imagined. We also saw a giant anteater with a very large bushy tail, and I learned that the word *aardvark* means *ant bear*. (Actually, it is kind of disillusioning to know that the first silly word in the dictionary refers to something real instead of an impractical sound.) Chuck called me over to see Ham, the chimpanzee who made the suborbital flight in the Project Mercury space program, and Laurie spotted Smokey Bear, complete with his costume, installed outside his cage.

Several huge tortoises looked old, wrinkled, and spent, with fat legs and feet like elephants. Bowlegged, their legs appeared to be put on backwards and their feet stuffed with balls of wadding. Walking in slow motion on tippy toes, they looked so primitive that they appeared artificial. One had a cast on his right front leg that was tied onto a wheeled platform, which gave him mobility during recuperation from some obviously debilitating but unannounced occurrence.

Gazing at the porcupines, I thought of an evening years ago when one of those creatures wandered blithely down the road past my parent's house in Dieringer, Washington; it left less nonchalantly when my brother turned the hose on him. We saw a gorilla that wasn't as impressive as Bobo in Seattle. At the express request of my all-male son, we went into the reptile house and saw several snakes, including a python that Laurie and I thought was too large for comfort. She and I left shuddering as we thought of him twining around us.

By far, the most fun happening for me at the zoo was the visit to the cathouse—that is, where the big felines live. We happened to wander in right before the noon feeding on an extremely humid day in the high nineties. The lions and tigers were just coming inside, so we went into the center of their large building to watch the proceedings. As the cats entered from their grottos, the keeper enticed them into separate cages around the periphery and quickly pushed the doors shut between them. Two tigers almost lost their noses trying to escape as the door slammed shut.

The keeper pulled out a large hose, switched on the water, and gave each big cat a turn at respite from the heat. The reactions were individual, and all were hilarious. The lions did their best to stay out of the way of the spray, even gingerly sidestepping the water on the floor. One especially wanted nothing to do with this activity, raising his nose as if to say, "This is beneath my kingly dignity. You force me into this plebian endeavor time after time. Don't you know I want no part of it?"

But the first tiger turned his back to the spray of water and sat there with his eyes half closed, a grin on his face, squirming his contentment. I thought of my own enjoyment in a hot shower. He didn't want it to stop, either. The tiger in the next cage sat down like the last cat, but then as he was sprayed, he rolled over and over on the wet floor. Then he jumped up and like a little kid playing a game, chased the spray around the cage.

Another lion was huge and ferocious; he was so fun to watch. His roar scared the crowd of people who had gathered to watch his antics. I kept encouraging Laurie to worm her way up to the front so she could see, but each time his growling began again, she would creep back beside me. There were so many people, and it was such a hot day that I just couldn't think of holding her up like I usually did.

This lion acted like he was angry at the water disturbing him, growling, roaring, and clawing at the cage as if to get away from it. Then he went back, got in the water, and played around in it for a while like a kid. Remembering that he needed to assert his terrible authority, he once more set up a rumpus, showing the sprayer he was not to be trifled with. He reminded me of a teenager who is mature one moment, asserting a right to be grown up, and in the next moment, once again shuffling his feet through the mud.

We especially enjoyed watching three tigers. While still together in a cage, they paced around and around, one after the other in single file. Every once in a while, one forgot to pace and stopped to look out at the people, and the next one in line ran into him. Then they straightened themselves out and paced in line again until the next one stopped and fouled things up. They were like a vaudeville act. Once they were separated into their individual cages, each one continued to pace, as if trying to push out the walls. When hosed with water, they lolled in the spray, rolled over on the floor, opened their mouths to catch the water, and then batted it away with their paws. When the water turned off, they got up and shook like dogs.

After the baths came feeding time; we were privileged to see this also. The keeper brought out a rolling metal cart piled high with huge hunks of raw meat. With a long-handled fork, he picked up a portion and stuffed it through a small area at the bottom of the cage. Just before the meat was placed in the cage in front of them, all the tigers reacted quite similarly. They paced back and forth, jumped around, clawed at the cage, and set up howls frightening to hear. The second the meat appeared within reach, the tigers greedily grabbed hold of it and pulled it inside so quickly I hardly saw what was happening. Once they procured their meat, each cat reacted in a different manner.

A couple of them quietly hauled their food up to their benches and calmly, with great dignity and no more hoopla, began to eat their meal. The very large tiger did not settle down when he got his food; instead, he roared and tore into it on the spot. Then he stopped and looked up suspiciously at several people in the crowd, as if afraid of a challenge to his right to this hard-won prize. One of the three stooges grabbed his own food quickly as it came through the gate, lay down on the floor with the meat between his paws, and just plain gloated. He didn't even start to eat; he just looked at it, glanced again at the people, and grinned in delight. He was very proud of himself. Watching him, I couldn't help grinning back. I imagine that, after a while, he quit showing off and began to eat, but by then we were off to do and see other things.

Oh, how delightful when it all turns out well.

5

STILL HITTING ZERO

*O*h, not again! Laurie's sixth birthday rolled around with a birthday party of neighborhood children. At the candle-blowing time, Laurie stopped, looked up at me with a hurt expression, and said, "You promised me a kitten when we got to Virginia." Hearing this, I was filled with chagrin and that special *failure-of-the-month* feeling reserved just for mothers when a little girl spoke up, "We have two little kittens to give away." When we arrived at the girl's house, her mother said, "The kittens are out in the shed. I'll try to catch one for you." We followed her behind their house to a dark shed filled with discarded furniture and junk. As we ventured further into this cavern, I slowly began to realize that the kittens had been born there, completely ignored, and never touched by a human.

I watched the lady call to the kittens and pull out drawers of old cupboards to see where they might be hiding. I thought, *Oh no, here we go again—what kind of pet would this make for small children? We had just been through a very discouraging dog experience. What company would a feral cat be for two small and extremely lively kidlets?*

We caught quick glimpses of the kittens as they darted about, prompting Laurie to say, "I want the pumpkin-colored one." We briefly saw an even more skittery black-and-white one. I felt sorry for the frightened critters; they no longer had a dark and quiet world but one with noisy monsters descending upon them, chasing them about their home—of course, they were bolting away in fright. Finally, just as I decided to find the courage to disappoint Laurie and back out of the situation, the lady caught the pumpkin-colored cat.

She thrust the cringing, trembling kitten at me. I took firm hold of the scared ball of fur, and we immediately started back home. I clutched the kitten, enclosing him firmly in my hands to prevent his escape, and saw only bits of fur here and there. Laurie was bouncing around us, eager to get her hands on her new birthday kitten. Of course, the neighbor children wanted to play with it also. I had to say no; I knew if it got away now, it wouldn't get back to its prior home, and, since it was so wild, it might not be able to find a new home, either.

When we got in the house with the doors closed, I let the kitten loose. It immediately disappeared. I scooted the neighbor kids away since the two noisy children who lived here were more than enough to scare the poor thing. We finally found him under Laurie's bed and that is where he stayed, except to come out at night for the food we set out. I figured if we left it alone to get used to the house and food, it would gradually get curious and come out to meet us. It was a period of relative quiet.

On the other hand, my two small lively children who love nature, animals, and people couldn't understand how a kitten could be afraid of them, or that it should be left alone to get used to its new surroundings. They wanted to play with it and give it love; they knew that a good lovin' was all that is needed in this world to cure anything. Leaving it alone was almost impossible, but we tried, and as time went by, the kitten gradually started moving around the house, although it never came close to anyone and fled as soon as someone approached—which, of course, was what the kids would do as soon as he peeked out. Then I started noticing an odd, muffled sound when he walked or ran, and it dawned on me that he was running in a strange way.

Again, a sinking feeling started to grow in the pit of my stomach as I imagined what might be wrong and why there was a strange sound with each step. Sure enough, by the time I was able to corner and capture the kitten—plus the courage to examine it—I found its legs and feet were deformed. The poor kitten had no back feet at all, and the front feet were only partly formed, with no claws. My stomach dropped, my mind raced, and I thought of future scenarios. How could it live as a normal cat? How could it protect itself? It certainly would never climb a tree (quite a handicap with all the dogs around), and, of course, I had promised Chuck a dog.

I continued brainstorming and imagined the kitten living as a pampered house cat for an older person without children, but I did not know if it could ever be tamed. It moved around the house fine and did not seem to be in pain. Then I thought, *Maybe it is so scared because it's in pain. So often when there are outer congenital problems, there are inner problems as well.* Carrying the thought further, I realized that with the added age and weight of a full-grown cat, more problems would undoubtedly present themselves.

By this time, I was concerned with more than just the good of the cat and its survival; I also needed to think about the children and me, and what we wanted in a pet. It was certainly not the kitten we had hoped for. Looking back later, I realized I also wanted us to be comfortable with a *purrfect* little kitten. So, what to do? What to do *now*?

I didn't feel I could take him back where we got him for two reasons. Anyone not oohing and aahing at a kitten's birth was probably not about to start now, so he would probably stay as a feral cat but with limited ability to fend for himself. The other reason was a problem I selfishly didn't care to face. In the way of life's ironies, the lady who gave the cat to us had a severely atrophied leg. How could I presume to face her and say that I didn't want the cat because it was deformed? Impossible to do.

So, with the kitten firmly in hand, if not my emotions, my integrity, or my courage, I declared, "The vet can take better care of the kitten than we can," and I headed for his office. As I look back to my own childhood of pretending to believe certain things to pacify parents, I realize my children also probably knew more than I told them. At this time, we were still hitting zero in this animal crapshoot, but our luck was soon to change.

6

BREAKING EVEN

*O*ur animal luck did change! The very next day, the vet called to tell us he had a nice healthy kitten for us. We hurried down to pick up a fluffy gray bundle who briefly became Dusty, then Smoky, and several other names until it finally settled into the name of Sasha, after the duck represented by the oboe in Prokofiev's *Peter and the Wolf.* He was very easy to potty train, which endeared him to me immensely, especially after the experiences we had been through. Already trained to a box, he easily made the next step to outdoors.

Sasha was definitely an extrovert; he was lively, friendly, playful, and thoroughly loved by four adoring people. Full of energy, he'd all of a sudden bound *de gallup de gallup* down the hall, seemingly intent on doing something very important needing his attention. Then, wham, he'd screech to a stop and give a puzzled look around, as if trying to remember the chore he'd set out to do. It was as if he were already showing signs of senility at his tender age. He would sleep just inside the open windows, on the dining-room chairs under the table as our first cat in Tacoma had done, or stretch out full length on the rug, looking like the diagram of a side of lamb.

Sasha liked to play with the leg of a pull-apart doll of Laurie's, batting it around on the wooden floors down the hallway and back. He intently stalked this prey as if it were alive, then pounced on it and smugly carried it off. He'd climb the rungs of the dining room chairs and then, hanging down, bat at a toy on the floor.

When I sat at the table to write or sew, he would hop onto the chair at the end of the table, walk across my legs to the chair at the other end, and turn around to retrace his steps. When he got a little older, he spent more time outside playing with Tiger—those two stalking, batting, biting, and chasing each other up and around the trees.

Laurie, always a loving and giving youngster, tuned into all the

Happy children and animals!
Chuck with our black poodle pup Kookla and Laurie with our gray cat Sasha.

animals, was thrilled with her new companion, and took good care of him. She also enjoyed the fun and attention returned from him. I might come across her sitting on the couch with Sasha and all her dolls in a semicircle in front of her, all of them intently listening as she read a story to her audience from one of her books. A very creative young lady, she would devise imaginative fun with all her "children." Cats, of course, were also for snuggling under the covers, dressing up, and carrying around in any doll vehicle available. With this roll of the dice, we found a winner ... yes, a definite keeper; Sasha was to give us love and fun for more than fifteen years.

While Sasha was still a little kitten and after many pleadings from one small boy whose sister now had a pet while he didn't, we decided something really must be done. Chuck said that he wanted a poodle, and I began to think that was a good idea. We definitely wanted a dog as good inside as well as out, for so much of the fun with animals lies in the evening entertainment and snuggling at bedtime. But oh, poodles

A family portrait with me holding Kookla, Chuck, and Laurie with Sasha.

cost money. Then I thought about how much money I had spent on Sparky, the *free* pup. That no initial cost had added up to quite a total. Why not spend the money initially for a fine animal and hopefully avoid paying it out down the line? (I have since found out that you can pay initially and later also.)

After looking through ads in the paper, we telephoned one lady from whom we learned a great deal about poodles. In fact, she was so into her subject she would not let me say good-bye. After an hour held as a captive audience on the lore of poodles, in self-defense, I started to say something while at the same time pushing the off button on my phone.

A week later, armed with another ad, Chuck and I and a carload of neighbor children set out for the given address with checkbook in hand.

While the rest of the children waited in the car, Chuck and I began our next dog adventure. We met a silver mommy, a black daddy, and six black baby poodles born eight weeks earlier. When I touched them, I was amazed at the feel; I don't think there is any texture as soft and soothing as baby poodle fur. It was more comforting than any fabric I have ever worked with. We looked into the puppies' eyes and both of us were immediately *goners*. We couldn't resist. The lady explained the registration papers to us. We would pick two names, send them to the American Kennel Association, and then find out which one they chose. She explained to Chuck that there would be a book that would list the dog's name and that Chuck's name as the owner would be there, too. How impressive to a little boy—and to his mother, also.

With our miniature black bundle of joy, we went back to the car with Chuck holding his new pup all the way home. You never saw a boy and his dog get so much attention. I was thrilled for Chuck. Always a caring young man, he had felt terrible about the experience with Sparky and missed him a great deal. He was never a demanding child or one out to get attention, and it delighted me to see him so happy in this situation.

What an experience! I couldn't help but look at that little roll of fur every five minutes and say, "Isn't he the cutest thing in the world?" (I realize I need to change my habit of calling any dog *he*, because this dog was definitely a she.) Chuck was a real good sport and let Nick and I name his new pup. We had both taken a couple of years of Russian, and we named her Malinkaya Chornaya Kookla, which in Russian would translate to *Little Black Doll*. Kookla did not need any time whatsoever to become very firmly a heart print in the Searle household. Another pet well done.

7

A PAIR OF ACES TO KEEP

Much to our delight and relief, Sasha and Kookla got along beautifully. They ate out of the same dish, ran up and down the hall, and played in, around, under, and over the chair rungs. When Sasha had had enough foolishness from this young pup, he would dash up the top of the black reclining chair. When the cat lay down on the throw rug to go to sleep, Kookla would rush over to promptly rest her head on the cat's stomach and go to sleep, too.

For a while, the dog stayed confined to the floor, not able to jump high enough to get on the chairs. I would lift her up on the couch to sit by my legs as I read or sewed, and the cat jumped up to join us. True to puppyhood, Kookla liked to nibble on a pair of shoes now and then, but, after all, what's a pair of shoes among friends? A few times Sasha clawed the recliner, but then that wasn't really tragic either. It took a while before our new little black doll realized that going to the bathroom casually around the house was not socially acceptable, but thankfully, she learned.

I had a beautiful decorator pitcher that sat alongside the couch on the floor. I had brought this two-foot-tall glass object 3,200 miles across the country in the U-Haul trailer from Tacoma. Sasha liked to bat at the leaves of the bamboo branch I kept in it, and several times during play, the animals knocked the pitcher over. I finally moved it up to a shelf out of their reach, but it was not a wise decision. There seemed to be more wind here in Virginia than in the Pacific Northwest, or maybe I just noticed it more with three doors open to cool the house. My pitcher noticed it, too; one day, this beautiful present from my sister got caught in the crossfire of a strong gust and toppled over for the last time. I was sorry to see it go; I was homesick for my family on the West Coast.

Sometimes a gale churned up. After a period of hot weather, the sky would suddenly cloud over, the wind began to frolic, and then thunder and lightning started. In this part of the country, you know—really know—when lightning descends. It comes from all directions, and here, there is no sitting, watching, waiting, and hoping to catch a glimmer, as in the Seattle area. It is not just a periodic zigzag flash at one point in the sky. No, solid sheets of light dance continually in all directions—with brilliant flashes so intense they seem not only visual but also visceral. I felt them. A few dimmer ones allow the sky to grow dark for a short time before the whole sky lights up again.

One night brought an especially impressive storm. The children woke up and coaxed the animals out of bed to come down the hall and climb into our bed with us, where we all watched the sky for an hour or so through our corner windows. The thunder rumbled continuously, broken only by crashing roars splitting the sky. We tried to determine how long the time intervals were between the lightning and thunder, but the very sharp booms and flashes all blended together. The phone also jangled every once in a while, either from wires clanging together or from lightning hitting them, I don't know which. The next day, when I asked the neighbor if things got hit from the lightning, the answer was "Haven't you seen all the trees with bark stripped off?" Ah ha, so that's why.

No matter how much clean water was in their dish, both animals preferred the availability of toilet water. A not-too-unusual sight was Sasha balanced on the toilet seat, with her long, gray-striped raccoon-like tail hanging down to balance her weight as she partook of the drink that refreshed.

Did we have humidity? Oh yes! There really is such a thing. It showed its ugly dampness in several ways: The sugar that cakes in the bowl, the saltshaker that doesn't shake salt, and flowers left in a vase that develop mold instead of drying out like they do in Washington.

The bathmat not only needed to be put over the edge of the tub, but also turned upside-down part of the day; both sides had to be exposed for drying to occur. Towels soured quickly, and the bedding was always clammy. Some days I just felt a little heavier.

Laurie reading to her dolls and Sasha.

I also need to mention that we moved into a brand-new house, not an older one. One day, when I was cleaning the bathroom, I noticed vegetation at the base of the toilet. On closer inspection, I realized there was actually a toadstool growing there. This was so strange that I left it to grow for several weeks as a novelty. Our bathroom plant didn't even need watering.

Every night, Chuck would toddle into bed loaded down with a much-grown black mound of fur. He not only took Kookla to bed with him, but he also tucked her under the covers with her head on the pillow next to his. Our bed linen may not have been as sparkling bluish white as in some other houses, but this warm, good feeling was much more important. Chuck did get a little indignant when I drew the line at giving only the boy a kiss but not his dog. Sometimes in the middle of the night, Kookla made a trip onto the red-and-pink-striped bedspread of the little girl in the next room. She seemed to know, in her doggy way, that cats are much more independent than dogs and that Laurie didn't have as much of a bed partner.

For a while, Kookla had traumatic experiences with people leaving the house. She didn't accept departures as stoically as Sasha. As soon as anyone donned a coat or grabbed keys from the counter, she would cry out loudly and clearly, rushing to the door in a heroic attempt to push herself out the door with us. When we came home, she barked excitedly and jumped up and down, becoming a danger to nylons.

Operation Discipline followed toilet training. We would call Kookla to the area rug, directing her to stay as we left. It took a while for progress to happen, and she never did like being left behind, but she gradually learned to stay so we could get out the door in peace and quiet. It was far more difficult to restrain her exuberance when we arrived home.

Poodle hair grows so quickly, and suddenly Kookla became a shaggy, unkempt miniature bear. I started to clip her with the scissors. Her body was fairly easy to do (although very time-consuming), but when I tried to do her face, her wiggling made me terrified that I was going to cut her. She was squirming and I was shaking; I soon conceded defeat and took her to the professionals. She received a puppy cut, which included her face, feet, and tail, while the rest was trimmed just a little. For the first time, she looked like a real poodle.

How differently her face looked with all that long straggly hair shaved off instead of hanging down her chin like a beard or over her eyes so she could hardly see! Officially trimmed like a poodle and looking like one, her attitude and demeanor also underwent a makeover. Before, she had been a bubbly puppy, rambunctious and full of the devil, and now she was a dignified lady with her head held high in a grown-up manner.

When Kookla was a naughty girl, I picked her up to put her outside. I would hold her back against my chest with one arm under her seat so she was sitting up facing outward. When I started to put her down, she would somehow shift her weight, and if I wasn't careful, she'd turn a backward somersault out of my arms. She was all black— her fur, her nose, her eyes. Only the insides of her ears were pink. Every once in a while when she ran, stopped suddenly, or swiveled her head sharply, her ears flopped back to show a spot of pink.

We enjoyed her for many years and one of her sons as well. Yes, we not only broke even, but we broke the bank with those two rolls of the dice.

8

WAITING FOR THE HURRICANE

I was used to the Interstate 90 tunnel on the west side of the Mercer Island floating bridge heading to Seattle, where, as kids, we thought if we held our breath all the way through, we would get our wish. With a short tunnel, this was an easy job. It is a very different situation with tunnels on the East Coast.

We lived in Yorktown, close to the mouth of the York River on Chesapeake Bay. A few times we wandered further afield, traveling south of Newport News and through the Hampton Roads Bridge-Tunnel to play in the ocean at the Virginia Beach Resort and visit the Cape Henry Lighthouse. This tunnel was not only much longer—three and a half miles—but down, down, down, and under the water. Our holding of breath was not for a wish but from fear.

We also experienced the Chesapeake Bay Bridge-Tunnel when we traveled north along the coast to spend a few days at the beach town of Cape May in New Jersey to visit a friend of Nick at the Coast Guard station. On that journey, along the northern edge of Virginia before entering Maryland, we passed two islands I would one day learn about. Many years after my sojourn east, I would teach with Jean Hill Chase, who lived on Chincoteague Island as a child while her grandparents lived on Assateague Island. Jean wrote a book of her mother's stories about growing up there, and I had the privilege of illustrating it. But that was to be a few years in the future.

Swimming in the Atlantic Ocean on the East Coast is different and more fun than in the Pacific Ocean. The water is warmer and the waves are more playful, picking you up and flipping you over and over. There seems to be no worry about the undertow we were always warned about on Washington State beaches. As a child on vacation every summer, I can remember being worried when my father would swim out beyond the waves and almost out of sight in the Pacific. But the ocean here on the East Coast is warmer than the rivers and even some of the lakes on the West Coast.

I was told that swimming here is much diminished in the middle of summer because the water gets so warm that it becomes infested with stinging jellyfish. The colored ones are dangerous, and I guess a single sting can make you quite ill. The white ones, I believe, are harmless like the ones back home, although I do remember at Campfire Camp on Vashon Island that some girls got stung by red jellyfish. I was always glad to not be one of them.

We swam mostly at the mouth of the York River, and a couple of times on very hot days, sudden summer storms would blow up. Dark clouds came out of nowhere, the sun hid, and the wind started whistling. It was, as my mother would say, a sight to behold. I called it *scurry galore*—dozens of people jumping up, throwing on clothes, and grabbing blankets. Those in boats pulled down their sails or paddled furiously to reach shore. Everyone moved as quickly as they could out of the sea, away from the beach area, running toward cars. At first, I laughed, likening the frantic scene to an ant colony—see all the little ants, see all the little ants scurry, see all the little ants scurry frantically.

But then I soon learned that leaving ahead of a storm is an official requirement. I suppose this decree was a safety measure to avoid the thunder and lightning and to lessen the number of needed rescues.

During one such time when a storm came brewing up at the beach, one of the windshield wipers on my car decided to fail. There was no room to pull over to the side of the one-way road leading away from the beach without stopping everyone else. The rain was as thick and heavy as water pouring out of a pan. Think of the sky turning as dark as dusk, and then no way to clear away the torrents of rain. The windshield looked as if a fire hose were aimed full force at it. My kids, with their heads out of the windows on either side, became backseat drivers who directed me right, left, and straight; I could see nothing. After several blocks, I reached a place to pull off to the side of the road and climbed out to inspect the faulty wiper. I thought it quite a considerate little implement to have only fallen off the window and not off the car. I clamped it on, it stayed in place, and as we continued, I was again able to see.

Since guests were coming for dinner that night, I stopped at a small grocery store to get a few ingredients for the pizza I was making. When I was leaving the beach, the blouse over my swimsuit had gotten damp, but just from running across the street into the store, I became completely soaked. I got inside the door just as the lights in the store went out. People were standing around as I made my grand sopping, unclad entrance.

As is often the case when I am uncomfortable, instead of becoming quiet, I tend to nervously speak out. I announced at large, "I don't usually shop this way." Of course, I immediately felt more stupid. From a practical side, I began to wonder if the electricity at home was off, and if so, how was I going to make a decent dinner for company.

At home, Kookla jumped into Chuck's arms as he came through the door, and we found Sasha hiding under Laurie's bed. My fears were confirmed—no lights, and thus, of course, no working stove. I had made the pizza dough in the morning and left it to rise while we were at the beach, so now I rolled it out, put all the goodies on it, finished making a salad, poured some wine for the arriving adults, and lit candles. Then we all sat down and played Monopoly for an hour. Then the electricity magically came on. I popped the pizza into the oven, set the table, served the dinner, and just as we sat down to eat, the lights went off again. We all thought that was very good timing and quite considerate of the electric company—I hadn't even told them that my dad was superintendent of the power plants for Puget Power on the West Coast.

Later that summer, we started hearing rumblings about the hurricane season. The 1964 Atlantic hurricane season officially began on June 15 and lasted until November 30, and it was slightly above average with thirteen tropical storms and seven hurricanes, five of which strengthened into major Category 3 or higher storms.

This was all so new to me. I now lived where there were real hurricanes, and we could possibly be in the path of one. Nick told me if one came close, he would have to stay at the base. I followed the warnings of various gales as, one by one, they were announced on the news: where they started, where they were headed, and later, where they petered out. I was amazed at how slowly they traveled from one place to the next, even those with tremendous miles-per-hour winds.

Two were supposedly coming very close to us with a strong possibility of hitting our area. Nick was called to stay on the base while I listened to all the warnings and kept kids and animals close by. Chuck and Laurie helped me prepare for the eventuality of the full force of an impending hurricane, while Kookla skittered around underfoot and Sasha hid. Like all animals, they seemed to know when trouble was expected. I checked for plenty of food on hand and water in the refrigerator; we moved all portable items inside and battened down whatever wasn't. I kept looking outside to see the state of affairs and realized that no one else in the neighborhood was paying attention to the warnings. Broilers, lawn chairs, hoses, flowerpots, children's toys, and various other homey outdoor living articles still sat visibly around the neighborhood.

This was the first time since 1886 and the last time until 2004 that three hurricanes would hit Florida in one season. One of those storms, Hurricane Cleo, killed 156 people in its trek from the Caribbean Sea across Florida, causing serious property damage totaling $187 million, before it weakened to a Category 2 storm. Only remnants of it were left when it reached the Virginia coast, where it dropped more than ten inches of rain. Norfolk collected more than fourteen inches in twenty hours from August 31 to September 1. Then later in the month, Hurricane Dora added more. Neither hurricane hit us.

I was reminded of Washington State's Columbus Day windstorm two years earlier. The National Weather Service picked it as the number-one top weather event of the twentieth century in Washington State. It was declared to be the strongest nonhurricane storm to strike the continental United States in the 1900s from Northern California to British Columbia. Winds reached 100 mph in Renton, Washington; forty-six people in all were killed (including fifteen in Washington State); and the equivalent of fifteen billion board feet of timber worth $750 million were destroyed. Tacoma in Washington State recorded wind gusts of 88 mph.

At the time, my children and I were living on Union Avenue on the back side of the College of Puget Sound (now the University of Puget Sound) when the winds struck. Our neighbor had a tree crash across his car. My daughter, who was four years old, danced to the door, opened it, and said, "I'm going out, Mommy. I want to fly up." I immediately grabbed her arm, declaring "Oh, no, you're not!" as I slammed the door. Many times, she had expressed dreams of flying, and we did love Mary Poppins, but that would be carrying it way too far.

Forty-nine years later, on April 27, 2011, in Alabama, Mississippi, Tennessee, Georgia, Virginia, and Kentucky, the deadliest group of tornadoes in forty years would kill nearly 348 people in six states. The National Weather Service received 137 reports of tornadoes that night, some as wide as a mile and with an impact only one in a hundred ever reach. The University of Alabama canceled finals and postponed commencement for three months (it didn't need the stink of Limburger cheese deposited in the radiators by students wanting to get out of taking tests this time, as those in my mother's college class had once perpetrated). The destruction ranged from Texas to New York with flooding and washed-out roads. A photo showed utter desolation in one spot: broken concrete steps in the middle of nowhere, leading to nothing. It was all that was left.

I learned that the average tornado is typically only 200 yards wide on ground, lasts for only a couple of miles, and reaches a top speed of 100 mph. But some of these tornadoes were a mile wide on the ground, lasted for tens of miles, and packed winds of more than 200 mph. They were among the longest-tracking tornadoes in history. Just plain living in this world of ours seems to involve a luck of the draw, and I was glad to escape all of them. Something was right this time.

9

FORTY-SEVEN DEGREES BELOW?

*O*n the East Coast, fall was long, warm, and thoroughly pleasant. It was often hot but without the humidity or duration of summer. Children and animals enjoyed playing outside. There was some fog and a chill in the evenings, but the days were beautiful with sunshine. I enjoyed having the doors open in November and December; what a wonderful and welcome fuel bill this kind of weather makes. An added bonus was the freedom of animals going in and out at will without my having to constantly open the door.

As the fall deepened, we started thinking more about home, the kids clamored to go back for Christmas, and I began looking into the logistics of train travel. I made kennel arrangements for the animals, bought tickets for us, baked many chocolate chip cookies (Grandma's recipe, of course), and packed sacks of apples and peanut-butter-and-jel-ly sandwiches. Since we were traveling on a very tight budget, I figured those would hold up without refrigeration for the duration of the trip. Nick would be on duty at the base, so Chuck, Laurie, and I set out on the first leg of our journey back home for Christmas in the Pacific Northwest.

The train from Virginia to Chicago was crowded, with no seats to spare. Many servicemen were traveling home to spend the holidays with their families. As we neared Chicago, several announcements warned of difficulties at the train station, telling us to be wary of people.

The year 1964 was a time of civil unrest with race riots breaking out in spots throughout the country. We had changed our minds earlier about visiting New York after the news reported turbulent hap-penings in Rochester and New York City. In Philadelphia, tensions had escalated for months over several well-publicized allegations by Black residents of police brutality. A race riot followed, and for two days angry mobs looted and burned mostly white-owned businesses in

North Philadelphia. The police were outnumbered, and instead of aggressively confronting the rioters, they withdrew from the area. No one was killed, but during the three days of riots, 341 people were injured, 774 people were arrested, and 225 stores were damaged or destroyed. A riot also followed in Dixmoor, Illinois, a lot closer to where we were now headed.

It doesn't take much to scare me, and I knew we had to change to the Great Northern Railway in Chicago. The station was a monstrous cavern without the nice, big, easy-to-read signs I wanted to find—those telling me immediately and exactly where I needed to go. I stood for several minutes, did a couple of 360-degree turns, and looked everywhere for an indication of what to do and where to go. Deciding I needed to branch out on my own for further information gathering, I marched the kids to an empty spot in the middle of the train station, plunked our several pieces of baggage down on the floor, and said, "Sit down on these. Do not get up until I get back. And … if anyone comes near you, scream like crazy."

I quickly walked up to a window, asked for directions to the Seattle train, retrieved my children and baggage, and we were off on the second part of this trek. It didn't occur to me until sometime later—what a way to instill fear into young children. I am sure they have learned through the years I often opt for expediency.

The train to Seattle had many empty seats with lots of room, and the children had fun exploring it without disturbing anyone. I had brought books and games, and as usual, we kept ourselves busy. We met a pregnant lady from Alabama traveling with two very small children to join her husband stationed in Alaska. She looked bedraggled indeed. We also met a college student heading home for the holidays.

The first night, the attendant asked if we would like a pillow. I said, "Yes, please." I took it, said "Thank you," and settled down with the kids for the night. He stood there. Then he continued to stand there. It took me a while to finally realize that he wanted a tip. My hayseed identity came into play—you know, the one that perches on my shoulder all the time but once in a while speaks up to remind me, *Remember now, you're just a country bumpkin. Don't you get too big for your britches. Don't you go pretending that you belong with those big-city ways—no, don't go getting uppity.* Not only did I not know anything about travel etiquette, but I did not have money for any extras. He finally went away.

In Fargo, North Dakota, with the train delayed, I stepped outside. What a surprise—it was forty-seven degrees below zero! I had never felt such a temperature before. My shins ached; my cheeks hurt. Taking a breath was painful and stung the back of my throat. I had read about such an environment, but descriptions in a book hadn't prepared me for the actuality. It was a La Niña year with a very cold winter, when the waters of the Pacific at the equator were unusually cool. The records say that thirty-eight days were colder than forty below zero in Alaska that year. It wouldn't be until December 4, 2016, that the 1964 record for one-day snow at Chicago O'Hare Airport would be broken. I do not like extremely low temperatures any more than I like temperatures over eighty degrees. I am a middle-of-the-road person; the Pacific Northwest suits me just fine.

On the train, we experienced slowdowns and stops. The first of many announcements informed us how late our arrival would be and the conditions causing the delay. Periodically we heard updates of more hours extending our arrival time. I worried about my folks waiting for us, and I hoped because of the extreme weather, they had thought about a potentially late arrival and were staying home as long as possible.

We offered some of our food to the college fellow who was without money and had not packed food for the trip. We did finally arrive, and not only did we have a great Christmas with family but also met our newest member—Amy Elizabeth Curtis, born three months earlier to my sister and brother-in-law. She was underneath the Christmas tree nestled in with all the presents when Chuck, Laurie, and I saw her for the first time. My children learned from my sister while she was nursing Amy that there is orange juice on one side and chocolate milk on the other. She undoubtedly pushed Santa Claus and the Easter Bunny as well.

10

SPILL-MY-GUTS TIME

After the holidays, our train trip back home reversed as we traveled through Everett, Wenatchee, Spokane, Whitefish, Shelby, Havre, Williston, Minot, Fargo, Minneapolis, and Saint Paul. Finally, we reached Chicago, where we exchanged trains again for the more crowded final eastern trek. Late at night, a busy family holiday over, the children tumbled into two adjoining seats and quickly fell into a deep sleep. I took the seat across the aisle next to a pensive-looking young sailor. Once again, the train was packed with servicemen returning to their bases after emotional visits with families and friends.

My children were taken care of for the moment, my own emotional family reunion was behind me, and sleeping bodies in all angles of recline and sprawl surrounded me. I seemed to be in another world. I likened the situation to the once-in-a-while car trip where closeness can open parts of the psyche seldom or maybe never before expressed or shared with another. The coziness of the darkened train; its soothing, rhythmic swaying; and the rumbling and clacking of wheels—all seemed to encourage such a time.

My sailor companion must have also felt similarly lulled by the motion, isolated in our nest of seats and shut off from the larger crowd, for after starting a conversation with the usual pleasantries, he began to share his thoughts about his visit home. He expressed feelings, wishes, and regrets of his life. He told me how painful his holiday had been and how he had never been good enough for his father. As he continued to open up, I realized this was an entirely new experience for me—no one had ever before so exposed themselves with me, or been that vulnerable, that honest. It was something I had wished for all my life with my own family but was never able to achieve. And I certainly had never been able to bring it about.

After some time, he wound down, looked over at my snoozing children, and asked me how I happened to be traveling alone with them. The atmosphere and the permission given to me by this stranger in the middle of night, probably combined with the impetus of having spent several days with my family, somehow allowed me to open up as never before and not again for more than twenty years. I undertook to tell him my story, surprising myself, for after my initial decision to flip the switch of sharing—always before stuck in the off position—I found myself saying things not only never before told, but never before acknowledged even to myself. Not until I heard the words coming out of my mouth that night.

I'm pretty humiliated about my life, really. Stupid choices. I was so unprepared and just plain didn't know how to grow up. Near the end of my senior year of high school when major life decisions needed to be made, I started dating Fred ("Fritz"), the father of my children, and as time went by, I built a fantasy of a lifetime with him. We were not in any position to be making adult decisions; both of us were missing several important life skills. I did go to college for a year but was afraid to branch out and kept going back to him. After several months, we started having sex. Two other girls in my college room were also having sex, so this seemed like a permission of sorts and also induced a warm feeling of belonging. Years earlier, I had asked my mother about birth control and was met with her usual tight-lipped non-answer. To me, this indicated birth control was not okay.

There was little in the way of straightforward answers for help or direction in my life. When I started my period, my mother's comment was, "I don't know why you girls are starting so early." I was glad I had; I wanted to be normal. Another comment was, "I don't know why your breasts are so small." I didn't know either, but that caused me shame. Anything related to sex seemed to not be okay. I came away with the misguided idea that if I were to live a normal life, I would have to go against my family dictates.

To both Mother and Daddy, the body was a vast wasteland of nonentity. Daddy relegated everything to the head. When I was sick, he'd say, "It's all in your head." Mother got a disgusted look on her face when she had to physically care for me. What *was* accepted?

Intelligence, book learning, grades—yes. Activities, producing, achieving—yes. All kinds of creative and constructive endeavors—yes. Talking about a garden and the aphids—yes. Travel, history, and things or times out there—yes. Feeling or expressing your feelings—no. Having a different opinion—a very definite no.

I wonder now if there is a genetic component at work here. I have heard quotes that the English are so embarrassed of feeling emotion that they seem dead, while the Welsh have the original stiff upper lip. My sister used to accuse me of being too sensitive until the day I turned back to her and said, "Well, I'd rather that than the opposite—insensitive."

One day, thinking about my fears, I asked her what she was afraid of. She quickly turned to me and said definitively, "I'm not afraid of anything." I thought, *Could that be possible or is it just a defense?* When I took my brother for his first chemotherapy session, I asked him, "Are you nervous?" His response was, "What's there to be nervous about?" Well, maybe my sister is right—maybe I *am* too sensitive. I certainly was for our family, anyway.

An interest in boys was ridiculed and put down by Daddy. It was obvious that neither of my folks liked Fred, but I had no idea why. With conversation, I might have learned something. With tight-lipped and grim-mouthed disapproval, I was left with the impression that whatever I did was wrong. I felt no direction, no avenue for change in what I was doing. I did not want to goose-step after my sister, so I quit college and got a job in Seattle.

I took a deep breath and told the young sailor, "Your sharing opened a floodgate of things I have not thought of before. Actually, I guess I probably don't do much thinking. I just *do*." The young sailor encouraged me to continue, so I did.

Maybe my decision not to continue college and go along with the teaching bit was an attempt at independence on my part. I was too easily affected by any rejection from others of my plans for activities.

I never felt wanted. My father was determined to have a boy, and my mother thought it rather uncouth to have more than two children (her father was one of fourteen). No girl's names had been chosen ahead for my older sister or for me. That gave me the message I was wanted only if I were a boy.

I always wondered if my sister Joan was who Mother wanted to be and if I was the part of her she would rather discard. My mother had several habit patterns I tuned into from childhood. She seemed to shuffle me over to my father; it was almost as if she were pushing me away from her. When talking about Daddy's family, she would look at me, but while talking about her family, she would look at my sister. Believing in doctors, she acknowledged my sister's mumps and had her tonsils taken out. Daddy did not believe in doctors and my mumps were not acknowledged; I still have my tonsils, along with the sore throats that accompany them. When my children had the mumps, the doctor tested me and told me I had also had it as a child—it was just not acknowledged. For one reason or another, I didn't seem to belong with the rest of my family. I kept trying to pedal faster to catch up without knowing where I was going or what I wanted. It was like trying to fill in a picture with a bunch of dots missing.

As I talked to the sailor, I reflected a little further and then added I wished I had grown up in a family like the one in *Little Women* where all the women stuck together. I wanted to belong with them. I wished I had grown up in a family that encouraged me to look ahead, to think and choose for myself—and supported me in pursuing what I wanted and figuring out how to get there. It never occurred to me such a thing was possible; it just felt like I was always told to do it "the family way."

I dated Fred for three years, was engaged to him for a year, and then I got pregnant and married him. Two weeks after our wedding, I found a note on his windshield from a girl and discovered he had been going out with her for a while. He was rarely home, life deteriorated, and when I was six months pregnant, my folks talked me into moving back home with them.

One day, when I went to the doctor, he looked at me and said, "Lady, you are having a baby—get to the hospital." Mother dropped me off outside the hospital and within the hour, I delivered. When my mother came later to see us, her response was, "If I'd known you were going to deliver like a cow, I would have stayed." My mother came from a family of dairy farmers.

In a few months, Fred started coming around again, and I moved back in with him and got pregnant again. But I soon saw the writing on the wall—Fred was not kind to his dog. If Chuck fussed during the night, he yelled, "Shut that kid up! I have to work tomorrow." He knocked me off a chair when I was four months pregnant with Laurie, and then I found out he was buying liquor for teenage kids. I didn't know how to deal with him, and I didn't want his behavior to escalate with my children, so I moved back in with my folks to deliver my daughter, again without a partner or help. This time I gave in to my folks, not Fred, and returned to college to get a teaching certificate in home economics.

I also began to realize my folk's side of the problem. I was not only humiliating myself but was also a disgrace to my parents. They lived in a company house, which exposed my situation to all my father's employees. I was the black sheep, a pariah of the family, and I mostly withdrew from my childhood friends for the next fifty years. I kept my nose to the grindstone, had no social life while going to school, came home to take care of the kids, and then studied through the night. After I graduated, I got my first teaching job, where I met the man I came to the East Coast with. And this time I was no brighter about men than the first time. I found out he was still married, and of course, he insisted that he would divorce and we'd get married. I am a sucker for sweet-talking attention; I needed to feel like I belonged somewhere, and it was my drug of choice.

Growing up, I did what was expected of me. There was no allowance for differing opinions. My relationship with Nick was great because not only did he tune into me with wonderful energy, but he also admired and encouraged my mind and opinions. Our conversations were energizing—we discussed and examined subjects of the world around us inside out and upside down with no defensiveness about opposing points of view.

Turning back to the sailor, my voice dropped as I continued weakly, "I thought we were going to be married. That hasn't worked out. I should have known better. Actually, it wouldn't have been good anyway; I am starting to realize he is not the best choice for my children either, and

I've decided to head back home. I haven't quite gotten up the gumption to make that step yet."

Then my voice became even quieter: "But I know it's coming."

With that, we settled back into our own reveries. Not only clueless, I was also clueless of being clueless.

Nick in his Coast Guard lieutenant uniform.

11

SNOW TIMES THREE

We arrived back home from Washington State in time to experience a second winter on the eastern side of the continent. Our Virginia neighbors said winter comes in January and February, and we found they were right. On three different Fridays, every other week, a blizzard moved in and lasted through Sunday. The first time, some snow still lay on the ground on Monday, resulting in no school. The next time, there was no school on Monday and Tuesday because it was the end of the semester. On the last time, the snow didn't last as long.

Oh, what fun we had! Sasha poked his nose out to explore, did a once-around to determine what all this fuss was about, and then retired to the house except for necessary excursions. He did not like to scratch through the snow to find a patch of dirt to do his business, and he quickly hurried back inside. Kookla was much more adventuresome and kept up with the kids in every activity.

The first snow was too powdery for Laurie to make a snowball stick together, much less the snowman she wanted to build. Not only was it not as wet as snow in the Pacific Northwest, but it just plain didn't hold together. But, being a very creative lady, not one to be easily daunted and never thinking in terms of the impossible, she came into the house, filled a pitcher with water, and went back out to add moisture to the dry snow. After slowly building a miniature snowman, she came in again, retrieved a small red chair, took it out to the porch, and plunked her snowman down on the chair. Kookla, of course, immediately put her paws on the chair edge, leaned in to explore this new creature, and then proceeded to lap at it for a drink.

Years later, my daughter would winter in an abandoned barrack on the Aleutian Islands, then build a log house on forty acres on the top of a mountain outside Tonasket, Washington. Yes, enterprising to the core.

The second snow was moister, and I had trouble convincing the children that snow in other people's yards is not for use by the general public. They didn't understand why they couldn't just roll up snowmen from yards all over the neighborhood. We kept an icicle brought in from the gutter in the freezer. It reminded me of the big snow and silver thaw in Snoqualmie, Washington, 1949 to 1950. Those icicles reached three stories down from the eaves of our house. They must have been a safety hazard; why weren't they broken off to avoid possible disaster?

But how beautiful the valley was that winter! We lived on the hill behind the power plant above Snoqualmie Falls, which were frozen over with giant icicles. Trees and wires were weighted down with piles of ice and frozen snow. The snow plowed into the middle of the roads in both Snoqualmie and North Bend was so high you couldn't see across the street.

Much later, in 1999, in a newspaper article titled, "Biggest and Baddest Storms in Northwest History," Jeff Renner wrote, "On January 13 [1950], a whopping twenty-four inches of snow blanketed Seattle, the second-greatest twenty-four-hour snowfall in the city. That January, there were eighteen days when the temperature never rose above freezing. I'm glad I'm not old enough to have lived through that month."

But I certainly did, for it was my first year of high school, which was closed for two weeks. I built snow sculptures of a man, a woman, and a child while my father built my six-year-old brother an igloo. The men in the machine shop at the power plant built a sled for him from scraps. It was great in theory; however, with no steering mechanism, it proved dangerous in reality. That was the year all the people from the Puget Sound Power and Light Company houses—grown-ups as well as kids—went sledding down a wide hill east of Snoqualmie Falls Lodge, just below the hamburger stand, from the upper to the lower camp.

It was one of those memorable, never-to-be-forgotten times when all ages joined together, giving no thought to barriers of any sort and just responding to the fun of the time. I remembered an article I had read a couple of years earlier in *Reader's Digest* titled, "The Day the Town Flew Kites." A whole village gathered to fly kites—I was so impressed I wished for a similar experience. Two years later, the sledding experience granted my wish.

The ice storm must have been terribly hard on the trees and bushes as well as on my father, who was in charge of the power plant at the falls. There was always difficulty during any extreme weather, and it must have been even more so then. Now for the first time, I also realize my mother's job. She put up with the continual mess from children barging outside, who were probably leaving the door open, only to tramp back in later with chunks of snow clinging to woolen material. We would spread our dripping clothes on old-fashioned registers and sit shivering in front of the heat reading while our clothes dried so we could go out again.

My own children in Virginia were also in and out—out and in. There was a vent in the kitchen floor where they dumped mittens and boots, and beside which they set a chair to hang snow pants, trousers, and jackets. Kookla, with snow stuck to her fur, tried to cozy up to the heat. It seems something happened to my personal thermostat since the days when the spread-out clothes belonged to me; I don't care much for long stints outside on my feet these days, much less rolling up snowmen and certainly not swishing around in the snow to make angels. When the water in the marsh froze, the kids walked on it while some of the

Kookla with my sister's glass pitcher.

A collection of nests, seeds, burrs, and other visually interesting bits of nature.

teenagers went ice skating. Of course, my kids wanted a pair of ice skates. I thought it impractical since there was very little frozen water in Western Washington. Little did I know that in 1972, when we moved back to Federal Way in Washington, we would ice skate on our very own pond, but that was to come later.

Something interesting occurred at this time. On the coffee table was an oval white bowl my mother gave me. In it were three glass balls of different shades of green, coordinating with the tall glass pitcher that blew over in the fall winds. To a little white bowl, I had added round green mung beans. In my design classes, I had learned to appreciate the color, shape, and texture of objects of nature as well as elements of design in abstract art. Rocks, beans, seeds, dried branches, fungus, shells, burls—all are wonderful sculptures. Those unacquainted with the study of art looked askance when they came into my house and saw these ordinary objects used to decorate without the ornamentation of painted designs. The daughter of a next-door neighbor who lived behind the marsh once came over and said she and her mother had seen a room of modern art at the Smithsonian with decorations similar to mine. Suddenly, she looked at my choices with a different eye, and I gained a new level of esteem in the neighborhood.

Acceptance is so wonderful—how I enjoy it when it happens.

12

A Disturbing Interlude

Kookla had great fun playing with her next-door neighbor, Cookie. Of course, the grown collie makes three of our miniature poodles, and their form of play consisted of our pup running circles around the larger dog and jumping up to try and get to the same level. Cookie had a bad habit of chasing cars, so when Kookla was old enough to be outside, we all watched carefully to see that she did not follow her example. Our diligence over a period of time led us to believe she wasn't interested in picking up such a bad habit, and so we relaxed.

Through the winter, with cold weather holding on, our new canine addition spent most of her time inside with us, but eventually the arrival of spring brought warmer temperatures and we all began being outside more. During March, the wind blew now and then. In April, the trees began to bud while daffodils showed cheery faces and the sun played games of hide-and-seek, more often shining than not.

One day, the children came into the house screaming. "Kookla's been run over! She was chasing Cookie chasing a car!" Looking out the window, I saw our little black bundle of joy lying two yards from the edge of the road, crying loudly.

I told the neighbor kids to go home, grabbed my purse and car keys, went out the side door, and told Chuck to carefully lift Kookla into the back of the station wagon.

A man, whose car was stopped down the road, was walking back to say that some children told him he had run over a dog. I replied, "Evidently, you did." Bent on the important task at hand, I did not take the time to commiserate with his bad feelings but later appreciated he cared enough to stop. By this time Chuck had the pup quieted down in the back of the car, and both kids were snuggled in with her. I climbed in, and we left for the vet's office.

Both children began talking at once, telling how suddenly Kookla had started chasing Cookie. With a sob, Chuck said, "She couldn't get up or walk." He added, "Maybe her leg is broken." And then, "Is she going to die? Will the vet keep her?"

I sheepishly realized where that had come from and replied, "The vet will save her. We'll see what he says." I was sorry to see that my fatalistic Irish attitude, well honed from several generations and previous animal decisions, had reached my children.

Chuck carried our trembling puppy into the vet's office, where we were immediately shown into an examining room. The vet gently felt Kookla all over, looked at her mouth, took her temperature, and said, "I can't feel anything broken, but often we lose more animals hit by cars from shock than from actual injuries. I'll give her shots to prevent shock and X-ray her to find out if any bones are broken." So, we left Kookla to the care of a capable and kindly vet and went home to a very quiet house. There was very little sleep that night.

The next morning, I called the vet. He told us, "Kookla has no broken bones but is vomiting, and I want to keep her another day." So, we spent another long day and night before he called to tell us she was okay, they would clean her up, and we could come get her. An anxious crowd of three picked up little Chornaya Kookla. Ever glad to see us, she gave Chuck's face several washings by the time we arrived home. She was, however, very quiet, slept a lot, or just lay there looking around with lethargic eyes. Still worried, we tried to convince ourselves the shots were causing her malaise. And that was evidently the case because within the next couple of days, she returned to her usual exuberant self and therefore, so could we.

13
ADDED BONUSES

*M*y drive each morning to Williamsburg along the Colonial Parkway was particularly pleasant in the spring, with a crisp, sunny atmosphere mingled with colonial quaintness. As spring progressed, the sun became warmer, and I enjoyed the increase in rain over last year.

I was working at the Institute of Early American History and Culture, an establishment in conjunction with the College of William and Mary. I had taught physical education and food preparation at junior high schools in Gig Harbor and Tacoma for a combined total of nearly three years, but here I was employed as a secretary under another secretary, various editors, and eleven PhDs in early American history.

One of my activities was to help proofread books to be published. After reading aloud such lengthy and scholarly tomes cover to cover, including "reading" every punctuation mark, I would never again forget where periods and commas are placed in relationship to quotation marks. The abbreviated term *peer quo* for a period within the quotation marks, or *com quo* for a comma within the quotation marks, still infiltrates my brain fifty years later each time I write one of them.

At this job, I was reminded once again about my early life growing up in a small logging community where I would forever after feel like a country bumpkin with that hayseed in my mouth, not wanting to be called down for appearing "too big for my britches."

Thus, I was impressed to join high-caliber company when I attended an annual joint luncheon of the Institute and the College of William and Mary and found myself sitting at the same table as Alfred A. Knopf Sr., the founder of that distinguished New York publishing house acquired by Random House in 1960. He would die in 1984 at the age of ninety-two. His son later left his father's publishing house to become one of the founders of Atheneum Publishers in 1959. The Atheneum was one of the places for which I would type correspondences from dictations recorded by the PhDs.

My work did not take the full day to perform, and I was told I could use the college's library when I was finished with my chores. I took full advantage of that privilege and enjoyed the information I learned during that time. Later, one of the scholars gave me a couple of books from that library when I quit to move back home. I was also allowed to be included in the hour-or-more daily coffee breaks where I could absorb the discussions held within that rarefied intellectual atmosphere; I was enthralled with what I was able to listen to.

One day I had a chance to show a very different expertise of my own. When the coffeemaker did not work, I was instructed to purchase a new one. I saw the plug was broken, went out to buy a new one that night, came in the next day, and proceeded to strip the wires back and apply the new plug. When the coffeemaker gurgled pleasantly, doing its job of making coffee for these esteemed, highly intelligent men, I chuckled pleasantly to myself. In my job as a lowly secretary, I had accomplished a simple repair job not one of them had recognized as possible, much less attempted. I hope I didn't gloat.

Later, I was included on a trip to a publishing house in North Carolina where I enjoyed seeing the inner workings of its printing process. In my home economics studies, I had experienced many interesting field trips to food companies and textile mills. It is so fascinating to see the workflow of the manufacturing process and behind the scenes of their complex systems—ones we can only imagine.

That day of watching individual letters of lead type get chosen and combined to form words and sentences that were ultimately shaped into pages and bound into books intrigued me. When I returned home, I drew a diagram of the printing process, using the formation of letters to create a thank-you card. I depicted the letters flowing along an assembly line and dropping down into a tray to spell out "thank you."

Later, I received a message from them telling me how clever they thought my art was and asking my permission to use it. I was thrilled and granted that permission by return mail. Later I wished I had thought to request a copy of whatever it was they were considering using it for. I never knew if they did use my art or on what it might have been.

Another job I had was to help the head secretary collate a periodical publication. This was a mindless but time-consuming task. On jobs like this, my mind gets busy figuring out how to simplify the process and make it more efficient. I thought back to that book I read as a child, *Cheaper by the Dozen*, where the father is an efficiency expert and works out a flow for all the chores performed by the twelve kids in his family. In the same way, I thought of ways to rearrange the sequence and flow of our collating to save steps and eliminate back-and-forth motions. When I informed my coworker of this, she was quite incensed I would think to change the way she was doing her job. She never warmed up to me again after that.

However, I often think back to that job with fond memories; it had a rarified atmosphere different from any other I was to be a part of.

After Nick and I arrived in Virginia by car, my mother-in-law flew the children east to join us. She had an exceptional mind and was a great conversationalist, and she and Nick enjoyed many intriguing and in-depth conversations. They had shared their remarkable brains for most of the night before she flew back to Washington. She wrote the following letter to me while we were still in Virginia.

> This new expression of yours, Dianne, is predicated upon the fact that you are living in an element of joy and intelligence, with the interchange of sparks between you and Nick. The finest brains can soon become solvent when exposed to no irritant, no challenging medium of equal or better quality. Our brains are of the type that must have questions to seek, answers to find, and be challenged by the rims, edges, and circles of our environs. Our expression needs to not just be kept unhappily alive but to be excited—that is what my silly old brain prefers to be.

Everything had come full circle a year and a half after arriving on such foreign soil. I had received pleasures and pains; validation of intelligence, individuality, and sexuality; and experienced the nightlife of officer's clubs from coast to coast. But, realizing marriage to Nick was not for me or for my children, I determined to break away and make the trek home. Had I learned anything about consequences for future actions? Or would I still just keep going like the duckling?

14

HEADING HOME

*D*uring the fall of 1965, the children and I made the long trek home from Yorktown, Virginia, to Seattle, Washington. This time, the trip was much easier physically since our furniture and belongings were handled by a moving company instead of my planning painstakingly how to fit everything into a small U-Haul trailer and my station wagon. This time, I put the back seats down, topped them with a mattress, and added a box with dolls, Parcheesi, Scrabble, card games, put-together toys, crayons, storybooks, and puppets. We added what was needed by an eight-year-old boy, a seven-year-old girl, and me for a week's trip in a station wagon across our continent. The little money we had was needed to finish a fifth year of college so I could reinstate my teaching certificate, so we slept in the car, and, of course, the children played there.

Dealing with emotions was a different matter. I had gone east believing I would be married and, for the second time, have that *fantasy* of a happily-ever-after life with a man. This was not to be. It would take more than a decade to realize the difference between childish make-believe ideas and adult realities and even more time to start learning the skills necessary for a lasting relationship. Oh yeah, I had to even realize that I needed to learn such things. Some of us take a long time to learn important lessons in life. For me, it was a very long time.

Oh yes, I should have known better and would find out later during this very trip that I could still fall into the same trap. But that comes later. For the moment, I was going home on my own to find a job and again build a home for the three of us. Well, plus two, with the animals.

Amid a flurry of activity and then periods of lethargic inertia, the Searle household departed the Eastern shores for the wilds of the West on a late Monday afternoon. Having lost a cat on the trek east, I resolved to ship one gray cat and one black poodle by railroad, but at the last minute, it became too much, too late, and too difficult to figure out how, so I blithely drove past the railroad station in Williamsburg, on through Richmond, and to points west with the two animals still in the car.

The points immediately west happened to be in the midst of a terrific thunder-and-lightning storm that continued all night and through all of the "mountains" Virginia and West Virginia boast about. My daughter had picked up a fear of thunder and lightning from her Eastern friends and was so worried about stopping in the rain and lightning among the trees that every time I got tired and tried to stop to sleep, she popped up, crying out, "Oh, don't stop! Please keep going." Even snuggling with Sasha did not diminish her angst. We drove through most of the night until, in the wee small hours, when Laurie fell asleep, I finally pulled over to nap in the car.

The next day in beautiful sunshine, we drove across West Virginia and southern Ohio and up into Indiana farming country, where we heard a lot of noise followed by a boom. We had a flat tire. Before I had pulled off to the side of the road, much less out of the car, a tanned fellow in the truck behind us also pulled over, got out, came up to the window, and said, "Where's your spare?" Zoom! Quicker than the tire had gone flat, it was changed. My wide-eyed son was impressed as he watched this man move in, take over, and do the job. As quickly as he had arrived, without any fanfare or even time for thanks, our Good Samaritan was gone. I thought, *this must be a hallmark of farming country.*

After traveling twenty-four hours from Yorktown, Virginia, to Gary, Indiana, we stopped to see old family friends. Pam's grandmother and mine had visited with each other while pushing our fathers around in baby carriages. Our fathers had grown up together, and we had grown up thinking we were cousins. It was good to see Pam, Gary, and their four children again and we stayed through the next day. I appreciated their hospitality and thought it quite commendable for them to put up with me, two children, a cat, and a dog.

I remember two things about that visit. Evidently, Indiana has an insect problem like Virginia, and while Pam prepared dinner, flies started gathering. Suddenly she stopped, picked up a newspaper, rolled it up, and stepped around the kitchen. Swat, smash, and bam!—she demolished all the flies. I was very impressed.

I used that technique later one buggy fall when teaching kindergarten—adding my own theatrics of "Take that, fly!" and "You can't get away from me!" much to the amusement of a room full of five-year-olds. I still employ the rolled newspaper, adding my own embellishment of a rubber band on the end. To me, flyswatters are such harbingers of germs, but with the newspaper, you can peel off the offending outer layer and throw it away, while leaving the rest to demolish another swam of unwanted invaders.

The second thing I remember was the newscast threatening a hurricane. There was a lot of wind but no bad repercussions, and we left Pam's hospitality to continue our journey. Throughout the early evening, we drove through Indiana, and later we stopped during the night at a truck stop. I always took my map in with me. Somehow that made it all right to talk with other people who were traveling by night and stopping for conversation and coffee to stay awake. South of Chicago, we pulled into a motel parking lot for a few hours' sleep.

When I woke up to resume our travels the next morning, I had not realized we would be on the Chicago Turnpike in the middle of going-to-work traffic. I suffered agony for miles and miles with no way to get off the road and fearful of bladder overflow and gas underflow. I think I counted fourteen lanes of traffic speeding at a mad commuter pace. I thought, *What will it be like later?* Some poor fellow was stopped by the wayside changing a tire. I just hoped that my poor weary bald tires would wait for the open country.

Plus, I did not know where I was. I saw a sign with several town names but no route numbers. All the roads coming east had been plainly marked with the highway number, so I had quit paying attention to the names of towns and cities. Now, however, for the first time, this all changed, and, of course, in the worst of all situations. I realized I should have turned to the map for Chicago instead of jumping from Indiana to Wisconsin. Afterward, of course, I could laugh and add that would have made for a more boring day. But at the moment and for quite a while, it was anything but boring. Panicky was more like it.

All of a sudden, a toll station loomed ahead of me. Aha, a person to help our situation. I asked which way for where I wanted to go. The unsympathetic little man insisted, "Pay the toll." I informed him that

I didn't know if this was the road I wanted to be on. "Pay the toll," he repeated. One more time did not bring a more fruitful response, to say nothing of a more sympathetic one, and I paid his damn toll. Then, without as much politeness as when I had started, I requested directions for the trek west. He responded, "Go back the direction from whence you came."

We continued for several miles until I was able to turn around, come back, pay a second toll, and eventually found a gas station. We made it without either running out of gas or running over with urine. I don't know which would have been worse—wetting my pants or running out of gas. Well, yes I do, but I sure wouldn't have wanted to stand at the side of the road waiting for someone to stop if I had wet pants, also.

All of this to get off that blasted road, which I didn't want to be on and had already paid to be on. *Mumble-mumble, blankety-blankety, stupid place, mumble-mumble.* Oh, it is so hard for me to be ignored and shut off. That continues to this day to be an extremely painful method of abandonment. I would rather take a beating than be disregarded that way. However, I do not know since I never dealt with a beating—just an expression. And yes, I do use many of them.

Forty years later, Richard would call them my Englishisms. The story of him is yet to come.

15

GETTING HOME

*I*t was fun to stop along the way, sweep out the car with our little hearth broom, and take the cat and dog out on leashes to walk, get water, and feed them. People would stop, do a double take, and look at our Washington license plates. We laughed and made up games of what they might be saying to each other. "Crazy people. What else would you expect of those Northwesterners? They must be out of their minds." Either we got used to it or we didn't attract as much attention closer to home. Maybe weird sights really are more common in the West.

We continued up through Wisconsin to see beginnings of green hills with little dairy farms nestled among their curves. It was such pretty country, but oh, we were so hot and so tired. Finally, in a little town named Eau Claire, we stopped for ice cream cones. Finding a lake, we left the cat in the car with a dish of fresh water, hooked up Kookla's leash, and took her for a swim. When she had her fill, we tied her to the fence railing and plunged into the cool water ourselves. My children are both excellent swimmers and love the water. It felt so good to three tired bodies.

My mother's family came from this part of the country, and my grandfather sold his dairy farm in 1909 to resettle with fruit ranches in Sunnyside, Washington. He was one of fourteen children, and I had brought the phone number of a sister of his who still lived in Hudson, Wisconsin. It sounded so good to be answered with, "Hello, Dianne, come right over and spend the night." She took us out to dinner, and when I mentioned she had not eaten any of hers, she made light of it. We spent another night in a real bed instead of the car and took off again the next morning. Later I found out she had cancer at the time and hadn't lasted long after our visit. To take in a woman, two small children, a cat, and a dog without notice was very generous, but doing so with the addition of being terminally ill and not even mentioning the fact was an extreme act of hospitality. My gracious mother had come from this stock.

We drove across Minnesota at night from the west side of Wisconsin to the east side of North Dakota. In Fargo, we stopped at the farm of another great-aunt. I remembered her fondly, even though I was a child when she had come for a short visit. I was in the fourth grade at the time and her warm nature had touched me deeply. Her eyes had looked directly into mine and seemed to welcome me with a feeling of being regarded for who I was, deep down inside. Now she welcomed us in her huge open kitchen, allowed us to take baths, and fed us a large farm dinner before we left reluctantly to head out once again.

Partway into North Dakota, we got another flat tire, but this time we didn't fare so well. On freeways, people just aren't as ready to stop and help. This was not a country road as before. I got out, hesitated, hauled the spare tire out, hesitated, got the jack out, hesitated, and still no one stopped. I thought, *oh no, I am actually going to have to do this myself.* Of course, Chuck didn't want anyone to stop; he wanted to do it himself. Eager to do the job, he started cranking the jack up under the car. I was so afraid of the jack slipping that I don't know if I was more afraid of him being killed or of killing his confidence by telling him he was too young and couldn't do it.

Even though he was quite disappointed, I was thrilled when someone did stop. It became obvious the man had stopped only because he thought he should, because we soon found out he didn't know what he was doing, either. Worried about my jack, he was finally very relieved to discover my spare wasn't any good—we had neglected to get it fixed after the Indiana flat. Another instance of those live-the-moment, oblivious-to-the-consequences thinking. He took us and the tire down to the nearest service station.

To our astonishment, when we arrived back at the car, there was Nick. I had called it quits between us when I left Virginia, never thinking I'd see him again. He had departed two days after we did and driven like crazy to catch up with us. Yes, I succumbed and gave in once again; I still didn't know any better! We got our tire properly fixed, and then we really had a crazy caravan. Nick was driving his Dodge pickup, pulling a little blue Falcon behind it, followed by us in our old ugly but reliable Plymouth station wagon (well, the workings of it were very reliable; it was just the tires continuously giving us trouble). Nick would treat us to motel beds for the rest of the trip.

Often with children involved, planning can be in vain. I found the toys and games I had packed to be meaningless. The kids played for hours on end with the animals, were silly with each other, and made faces at people in other cars, but they didn't touch the games. When Chuck was in his forties, I heard about one form of their traveling entertainment. Making sure I was busy driving, they reached into our huge bag of dry dog food and threw pieces out the window, watching to see the reactions from other cars or pedestrians.

The greatest fun was when they dragged out the puppets to create shows for each other. Laurie wanted to include me, but of course, whenever we were in the car, I was driving. They would rig up a blanket with the ends rolled up in the windows on either side of the car. This provided a curtain for their stage. They would then tell me to pull down the rearview mirror until I could see their stage at the top of the front seats. Then they proceeded for hours to put on puppet shows, which I would see by periodically glancing at their endeavors.

The children took part along with the puppets, and of course their pets were included. It is wonderful how little it takes to amuse creative people. I once heard Ralph Nader tell on a talk show that when he was growing up, there were no toys. Kids were instructed to use their imaginations. That certainly seemed to work for them, and yes, it did for my crew as well.

When we reached the hills of the Rockies, the kids rolled up the mattress inside the car to sit on it, so when I braked for the steep declines, they could tumble off. I am glad this was before the days of seatbelts—how horrible to be restricted to sitting in one place all the way across the country. It was bad enough for me to be restricted to one position and I was nearly thirty years old. I know—terribly dangerous and foolhardy—how did we survive?

I also kept a journal of our travels both east and west. On the way back, we made sandwiches. Those majestic Rocky Mountains were so good for my soul after more than a year of modest East Coast hills and several recent days of tumbleweeds, sagebrush, and flat wheat fields. The mountains in the northern neck of Idaho were so different from the flat, dull, southern part we had driven through on the way east. On the last trek of this journey, I likened the north-south disparity of Idaho to the east-west topography of Washington as we rolled through the flat desert land of the eastern side of the state and into the wonderful Cascade Range outside the Seattle metro region. Here were rocks, streams, and honest-to-goodness evergreen trees.

My kind of land. Oh, how beautiful. At the foot of the Cascades, we stopped in the Snoqualmie Valley where I grew up. My heart still jumps up into my throat whenever I spot Mount Si. After all the country I have seen, this valley is still the prettiest to me and it still takes my breath away and brings tears to my eyes, especially after being away. How could anyone grow up in this spot without a love of nature and its beauty? On to Puget Sound.

I probably need to emphasize the differences in times and practices of when we made these cross-country trips from those of today, the difference in my philosophy, and the wide-open spaces without the constraints of our current car population on the roads. There were no such things as seatbelts back then, I had never heard of one, and there were none in my car. I would learn later that they came into being around the late sixties or early seventies. The first mandatory seatbelt law in the nation was in New York in 1984, and by 1990, thirty-seven states had enacted laws for mandatory seatbelt use.

Also, I have been less directive in child- and animal-rearing than many people. I have always encouraged initiative, independence, and creativity in both. I know that many people like to order and direct more than I do. I add this because I am sure there are those who would declare my actions dangerous and not always the best. As Nick would say, "So be it."

Needless to say, we all made it back to Seattle safely, and Chuck, Laurie, and I were still alive and well fifty years later. Sasha remained with us for a long time, and Kookla gave us not only many years of companionship but a litter of puppies as well.

16

SEATTLE INTERIM

After reaching the West Coast and spending a couple of days visiting with my folks, I looked for housing near the University of Washington. Settling on a place in the Wedgwood area at 2556 NE 83rd Street, I directed the moving van to deliver our goods. After enrolling the kids in the Wedgwood Elementary School—Chuck in the third grade and Laurie in the second—I registered at the University of Washington, signing up for seventeen hours to complete my fifth-year requirement. That was quite a load with two children and new responsibilities as the Blue Bird assistant leader and a helper with the Cub Scouts.

I am not sure when it occurred to me, but when it did, I was very amused. I remember saying as a child, "If I have to live in a garage, I will live where my children have others to play with." I had grown up in company houses above power plants with few other people within miles, and nowhere did I have children my age to interact with. All my friends lived close to one another several miles away. The only person near my age was always my older sister, and I missed out on a playmate with a more equal give-and-take. Now, I laughed at the irony: The rental I found for us was an actual garage.

This remodeled garage provided very small but adequate living quarters for the short time we were there. The front door opened into a small living area with kitchen facilities at the end and small bedrooms to the left. Kookla and Sasha settled in nicely with the children and me until we came home after a night away to find our cat with a neck torn apart and gaping open.

Sasha looked up, her appealing eyes saying, "Please help me." The neighbors came over and mentioned a fight with another cat. I don't know when I have been as angry as I was right then—they had sat there knowing about our gravely injured poor cat without taking him to the vet. I gathered up our suffering ball of gray fur and, without saying a word, took him in for surgery and antibiotics.

Then I discovered I was to perform treatment for a period of time. I had not known that animals heal in a different manner than we do. According to the vet, I had to keep her wound open and treat it while it healed from the inside. Despite my squeamishness at playing doctor, I survived the ordeal and Sasha healed nicely to survive for many years.

What happened with Kookla was much more fun. As a registered miniature poodle, she had been in heat before but was a very discriminating little lady who kept her bottom glued tightly to the ground. Here, she met another registered black poodle who looked just like her, fell in love, and let hormones take over. I understand that.

After the prescribed time, she delivered babies on Chuck's bed. Kookla did not take as naturally to motherhood as our later pets would, and she needed to be encouraged to feed and care for her puppies. No amount of coaxing would get her to accept the runt of the litter. She picked it up in her mouth and jumped down off the bed to deposit it at the outside door. I have often favored the downtrodden, so I took it back to her, foolishly thinking I could talk her into accepting it. She had made up her mind, and time after time, she dropped it back at the door again. I cuddled it and tried to feed it myself with an eyedropper, but I did not work out as a "poodle mama" and, to my disappointment, it died.

Kookla had always been an even-tempered dog, not at all like the pampered or temperamental poodles I have heard about or other small, yippy-yappy dog breeds, and I was quite surprised by her reactions. I don't know if she didn't really like the job or if she was missing some natural instincts and didn't know what to do, but right from the start, she was skittery with her babies. I once kept Chuck home from school two mornings in a row to stay with her until I could get back from an early morning class I couldn't miss. Chuck's principal did not think much of my action, but I knew Chuck was able to miss this time. I liked that my message to the principal stated the importance of family as well as that of education.

Laurie's school writings reveal, "On the fourth of February, we took the puppies outside for the first time for a romp." Laurie was to choose a little male to keep. She named it Peppy, and we were to have him for well over ten years. My sister reported in later years that the female she named Marinka was the best gift we ever gave her. Poodles are nonallergenic and the only dog she could have. We gave one pup to a friend of Gran and Gramps, only to find out later that person decided not to keep her and had her put to sleep. I was so unhappy over that information—I would have taken her back had I known.

I decided to do a class paper on information gathered from my stint at the Institute of Early American History and Culture in Williamsburg, but I needed to do some research. I found a University of Washington library on the campus map, walked into it, and looking around, saw nothing that looked familiar in the way of a library. It was a huge room, all paneled, with no reception desk and no signs indicating where to go or what to do. It looked like an exclusive private club. Puzzled, I left and went home.

The next day, I repeated the attempt. The library still looked exactly the same—no human in sight, no directions, no books to be seen, not even a sign on the wall. Again, I turned around and walked off the campus. This time, I climbed into my car, headed for Pacific Highway South, and drove the thirty miles south to the University of Puget Sound (UPS) I had graduated from and the Tacoma Public Library. These were libraries I was familiar with—ones with people around to answer questions, ones where I could see books on shelves. I found the information I needed and drove back to our little garage home.

I never did go back to that UW library to acquaint myself. Looking back now, I wonder if I had been in the wrong building, or maybe I went in the wrong door. Whenever I think about my misadventure, I think I should have gone back at some time to check it out. I still should, but it would be very changed after forty years. Sometimes I'm a bulldog and sometimes I'm a mouse. That time, the mouse won.

I finished my fifth-year requirement and was working as a temp for Kelly Girls to put food on the table while waiting for a job. Back when

I had graduated from UPS, my sixth-grade teacher and principal, who knew my father from Kiwanis in the Snoqualmie Valley, called and asked if I would like to work for him in Issaquah. At that time, I had become used to Tacoma and had already accepted a job there at Mason Junior High. It is so strange the way things go around; this time, while applying for teaching jobs in the Puget Sound area, I was hired by this same man, who was now personnel director for the Federal Way School District.

I also started looking around for a place to rent, although what I really wanted was to build a house; I had spent years getting to sleep at night by designing home floorplans. At this time, there was no such thing as an apartment in Federal Way, and I could not find a rental either. So, I started looking at houses to buy.

One house was in the vicinity of where Illahee School would later be built. It had several fruit trees and a chicken coop. The kitchen was ideal; it was big with a wall of windows looking out on the back pasture, the Cascade Range, and a great view of Mount Rainier. The property had only two bedrooms but met my two requirements—at least two acres and a fireplace. It was priced the same as the house I did eventually buy, but for some reason, the financing was arranged differently, and I couldn't get it. I have since tried to find where it was, but I think it went the way of "get rid of the old to make room for the new."

There was another house I was glad later that I didn't get. It had a little more character than the others and I believe its uncleared land extended to a lake, but there was no pasture for a horse, and it was close to the junior high school where I would eventually work for thirty years. I was glad I had not situated in the middle of where my students lived.

The one I eventually bought was not only right around the corner from an elementary school, with two acres, a fireplace, a pond, and a small woods, but it was also in an area where all the other houses sat on two acres, plus there were three lakes close by.

This decision turned out to be a good choice. It was great for kids, pets, and a nature-loving mother. It was never questioned with "Why didn't I know better?" or "What should I have done instead?" Instead, it proved to be a keeper for over fifty years. After Gran and Gramp's approval, in March we moved in.

17

Our Sky Fell In

"So, she hurried along and hurried along, and in a little while she met Cocky Locky." My daughter's eager voice chimed in with her part of the play my Blue Bird group was rehearsing in our home. "Cock-a-doodle-doo! Good morning to you, Henny Penny, and where are you going this fine day?"

Ravonna as Henny Penny cried out, "Oh, deary me, Cocky Locky! It isn't a good morning, and it isn't a fine day! I went into the woods to gather nuts, and a piece of the sky fell on my poor bald head, so I'm on my way to tell the King the sky's a-falling."

Laurie chimed back in, "Oh, what a dreadful thing! Cock-a-doodle-doo! Do you mind if I come along with you?"

All heads in the room turned to the door as my nine-year-old son burst through. Gulping back a sob, he yelled, "Mom, you've got to come! Kookla got out and was hit by a car!" After I confirmed he had put away the horse he had ridden to his 4-H meeting, I turned around and told Laurie to call Kay, who lived two houses up and was the mother of two of the Blue Bird girls meeting here. I further admonished, "No one goes anywhere or gets into anything, understand?" Laurie gave a very grave and sorrowful nod, and I added, "I'll be back as soon as I can." Grabbing Chuck around the shoulders, I led him out to the car.

As I drove up the driveway, I asked, "Now, where exactly is Kookla?" He sobbed, "Right at Meridian. I had just crossed Meridian when I heard her barking. I turned around and there she was, running to catch me. I couldn't stop her. There was no way I could stop her. Then a car on Meridian hit her." He raised those big liquid brown eyes to me and said, "And the driver didn't even stop. She went flying through the air. Mom, he didn't even stop to see how Kookla was! He didn't even care."

We pulled up to the spot where Kookla, now lifeless, had been thrown by the side of the road. Chuck gathered his wonderful little

Chuck with his beloved Kookla.

poodle into his arms, tears sliding down his cheeks. As he climbed back into the car, he buried his face in her soft black fur. Oh, that beloved ball of curly black.

As I turned the car around to head for home, Chuck continued, "There wasn't anything I could do. I couldn't leave the horse out on the road. And, Mom, I'm sure I put her in before I left." I told him he had indeed done just that—I remembered it. I said, "One of the girls must have let her out when they came in." I added, "I should have locked her up in your bedroom." *Wise thoughts after unwise actions do no good,* I thought, as my stomach churned with my own pain and guilt. I added that to the empathy I was experiencing of my son's pain.

This little pedigreed miniature poodle had been chosen on the other side of the continent as an eight-week-old ball of fur. She had traveled with us in our old Plymouth wagon all the way across the country from the tideflats of Virginia to the Puget Sound in Washington State. Not the best mother in the world, she hadn't always known what to do with her pups. (There are many of us with that problem.) But she had wiggled her way across a room to greet us, and she had wiggled her way into our hearts. She had been a wonderful companion for her master. At

Fritz during his visit to bequeath Duchess to us before continuing on to Alaska.

bedtime, she had climbed up on Chuck's bed, snuggled down under the covers, put her head on the pillow, and waited for him to come to bed.

Swinging down the driveway, I told Chuck I would take the girls home and we would plan a burial for Kookla at the side of the back pasture near the woods. It was a very sad and subdued Searle household that night and for some time to come.

So often, it seems that things fall into a needed place of their own accord. Some would say it's fate's decree. Whatever the rationale put to it, sometime after our tragedy, we received a call from Gran to come for dinner. Fritz, my ex-husband and the father of my children, was traveling from his farm in Trout Creek, Montana, to Valdez, Alaska, to run a fishing charter boat and was visiting his folks on the way. He had his dog with him, couldn't take her to Alaska, and asked if we wanted her.

Duchess was part shepherd and part coyote. She was a sweet and delightful gift, and we readily accepted her. She had led an exciting life of fishing, trapping, and hunting in Montana and would live a more sedate existence with us before dying of old age some ten years later. One pet doesn't take the place of another any more than a person can. But she helped ease our pain and fill in the gaps left by Kookla.

18

LITTER LETTER FROM GRAN

After the arrival of Duchess in our household, I dug through correspondence from our time in Virginia and found a delightful letter Gran had written to the children two years earlier about our new family member. My mother-in-law, a remarkable lady who would always be important in our lives, kept us in letters while we were away. She and my ex-stepfather-in-law, Shelly, lived with their two horses on acreage just outside of Issaquah on land under a pole line and beside a creek. Now, years later, we were the glad recipients of the delightful pet described in her letter.

Dear Chuck and Laurie:

August came around before we had any summer. Fritz came over to visit us and stayed for a month. He brought Duchess, his lovely little German shepherd. She had a litter of eight adorable pups while they were here. You would have been enchanted with the way she did it. I shall try to relate it as it happened.

Duchess is a very sweet little three-year-old part-German shepherd, part-coyote female dog from Montana. She lived in the wilderness for three long and very cold winters and knew the direction and love of one master. From the time she was a small puppy herself, she lived outside in the heat of torrid Montana summers, cooling herself in a small stream or escaping exhaustion in the cool afforded by slinking under the old house. In the winter she would find warmth under that same old house, and she has used great, fun-full mouths of snow for her water in the freezing times.

She is a hardy little dog—kind, loving, and friendly. She does not have many friends, for she does not know many people, but when she was very young—two months old—Gran and Shel went to visit her, and she popped her little brown head up through a hole in the old porch like a gopher looking out of its hole. We coaxed her out, and she came to know us.

This summer, as a very dignified lady planning to have babies, she came to visit us. She quietly took her place in our lives. She obeyed her master and us, for she knows how a good guest deports herself. She stayed close to the trailer-house as though it had always been her home. Everyone who came to visit exclaimed, "What a wonderful little dog: she is so well-behaved." We were soon to see how much!!!

Two weeks after she arrived, we could tell that she was soon to become a mother, and so we began to help her become strong enough to feed the little puppies that would be coming. We gave her much milk and even cottage cheese!!! Did she like cottage cheese! I hope you do, even though Chuckie will probably never become a mother! One of my little jokes, Chuck.

On a Monday night, Duchess seemed more affectionate than ever to her master and to Gran and Shulgun ... it was as though she were trying to tell us something. Being just people, however, we all simply patted her on the head as usual and said, "Time to go out now, Duchess," and we sent her to bed.

On Tuesday morning she was not at the door, sitting up as she usually did to say, "It is time for my breakfast." Everyone was in bed, except Gran, who usually fed her and loved her and enjoyed her for a little while before she (Gran, that is) had to go to work. I called and called her. Then I decided that she was just off for a little run up the hill. But she was too heavy to run very fast or far that Tuesday.

We all pretended to each other that Duchess would be all right and pretended to forget that we had all heard the coyotes calling the night before. Shelgun and Gran went off to the big city to work. Usually at work we are too busy to call home, but that day, for one funny reason or another, we kept finding time to call home and talk to Fritz. When he did not say anything about Duchess, we knew she was not at home.

That evening and Wednesday morning and again that night, we all called once for the Duchess. Then we began to pretend again that she was all right and that we were not worried, but each of us carried a great big load in his or her heart, and no matter what we did, it was there with each of us. Yes, we had visitors; even Mrs. Mattes and her two dogs came up and they yapped as usual (the dogs, that is), but never a sound from Duchess.

By Thursday morning, Gran had to say something like, "Well, do you suppose that Duchess went off up the big hill to the back and maybe the coyotes or a bear tangled with her, and she is hurt? It was just like when a flood of water happens ... for Fritz, Shelgun, and Gran all began to talk at once. We had already, the night before, called all the neighbors, telling them if a little German shepherd who looked like a coyote happened to go by, just call us and we would be there immediately ... what on earth could we do at this point?

Shelgun and Fritz had to take a truck that day, Thursday, and go up to a town called Darrington to load some lumber for the Children's Home. Gran came home that evening and got her supper and had to go to a Saddle Club meeting, but each minute that she was home she kept a keen eye and a sharp ear out for any sign of dear Duchess. No signs.

At ten o'clock that evening Gran came home from the meeting. Fritz and Shel were home and came rushing to the door to greet her. "She's here! She's here!" they cried together, and we all jumped together and hugged. And a couple of tears slipped out.

The trailer is set longwise of a creek, us you know, and there is much brush on the other side of it, and some on this side of the creek. It seems that the brush is thicker on our very own side of the creek than any of us had thought. For a miracle of nature had happened, and within eight feet of the trailer, hidden so beautifully by Mother Nature and God, there is a large old hollow cedar stump. When Shelgun and Fritz had driven in that evening, the proud Mother Duchess greeted them in the driveway, just as though to say, "You were not worried about me, were you? I was not worried over you, for I had a very large job to do, and it is done now ... come, I will show you."

With that, Duchess led us through a tangle of overhanging maple into the snuggest maternity ward we have ever seen. There *was a log over which anyone must go to gain entry to the big hollow stump (so that a good mother could have a warning while looking out for her young). Inside, behold! Eight of the most wonderful and wiggly little rascals you can ever imagine, let alone really and truly see! With flashlights, we peeked and tried to count these little bodies. It was a wonder. Then, crawling, muddy, tearful, laughing, we all came out and gave Duchess a hug and a kiss apiece and then gave her what she wanted most of all—a very large supper.*

Now the puppies are eight weeks old. Two weeks ago, they were all weaned. Fritz returned to Montana to take care of his cows, feeling better after spending time in an atmosphere of love and fun where everybody cares about what happens to each other. We kept Duchess and the puppies until weaning time. Fritz wanted two of the pups and, by that time, Gran and Shelgun could have wanted all eight of them. But we had to be strong. We found good homes for five of them; took Duchess and three with us and made a very pookie-pup trip to Montana.

We kept the "Giant" of the litter, a very lovely female puppy. She loves Gran and Shel, but we suspect she loves "Cross-Eye" the Siamese much more. Each morning, she feels it her bounden duty to give Cross-Eye a bath of love, and that dignified one-year-old cat secretly loves it. Tonight, they ate from the same dish. Our rugs are not spotless and our floors need more frequent scrubbing, but there is something going on here that is good for everyone. This is all we know to call this a happy ending to a story.

Love from Gran and Gramps

We were to enjoy Duchess's lovely quiet nature for well over ten years, paralleling the time that Peppy, one of Kookla's sons, was with us. Duchess had puppies here also, and true to the wild part of her nature, she took herself off when the time was right and had the pups under the neighbor's house, which was vacant at the time. After they were all born and doing well, she brought them home for us to admire and help care for before we found homes for them.

19

OTHER PAINS

*W*e found not all gifts should be automatically accepted. Around this time, Gran and Gramps offered us Two Toe. My mother-in-law not wanting this cat should have clued me in. They always had cats (often Siamese) and always with strange names. But this cat was offered to us, and since I grow too soon old and too late wise, too often, we accepted. But we did not become enamored with Two Toe. Years later, my son insisted the cat's name was DC, but I think he was influenced by the movie *DC* for Damned Cat after we had put up with some of Two Toe's antics.

After playing the piano, either my daughter or I sometimes left the keyboard exposed. Many times, in the middle of the night, we were awakened by the cat tromping up and down the piano keys.

During the time I finished college, my children and I lived with my parents for a little over two years. I was completely focused on getting a degree to become independent and, with almost no social life, the children were not familiar with the other set of grandparents. When Chuck was three and Laurie was two, I was determined to remedy that situation and we took the ferry to visit Gran and Gramps on Bainbridge Island.

Gramps, who was having trouble replacing the kitchen counter with a blowtorch, was muttering and mumbling. Chuck, always tuned into his surroundings with regard for others, walked up to him, pulled on the bottom of his shirt, and asked, "Having trouble, Man?"

He then saw an Italian blown-glass clown on the table. With those always serious, always beautiful big brown eyes, he pulled on Gran's blouse and said, "That clown would make me feel better." Well, no surprise; it immediately became his, but it stayed with Gran until years later when we were all settled in our own house, and it came to sit on the piano. There it became easy prey for our new midnight prowler. During one of Two Toe's piano tours cruising up and down the keys

Laurie, with Two Toe, Christmas 1967.

with an original tune, she ventured further up to knock the clown onto the floor, causing it to lose a few fingers and its head. Also broken were two candlesticks my father had carved.

Although she was not my favorite animal, I really would not have wished for her demise, but Two Toe came to a very unfortunate end. One warm summer evening I was going out to meet some friends. Sitting in the car with the window down, I was chatting with the children and their babysitter in the driveway before I was to leave for the evening. While we were visiting, I started the car. We had never been around an animal that did not get out of the way of a vehicle with its motor running. We had not had Two Toe for long, and it never occurred to me to check for a cat under the car. I started to leave and heard the children screaming. I had run over the cat.

I stopped the car, got out, and was horrified. The cat was in terrible shape. Obviously, no trip to a vet would help this time, but he was not dead. My son had already gone into the house and come out with a .22-caliber rifle Nick had given him. I was glad Chuck had just finished the full course of rifle-training classes he had been eager to take.

We were glad for Two Toe that Chuck had his rifle.

Even though we did not have the emotional attachment with Two Toe as we'd had with our other pets, I felt sorry for the sad chore this youngster had stepped in to take care of on his own accord. This was a child who had come into the house crying two years earlier after accidentally running over a snake with the lawn mower. Okay, another lesson—always make sure no animals are in the way.

Shortly before this incident, Chuck and Laurie had spent two weeks with their dad in Montana. Nick and I went to pick them up. Coming back on the interstate in the same Plymouth wagon we had made those two trips across the continent in, alongside a dude ranch near Cle Elum, we felt a terrible impact. A large object hit the right front of the car and seemed to slide along the side, and we screeched to a stop. My stomach sank with fear when I considered the possibility of that object landing in the rear seat with my children.

It took a few moments to gather my courage, turn around, and investigate the back seat. Chuck and Laurie were both visibly shaken with wide-open eyes but not hurt. A huge deer was writhing in agony alongside the road. Thankfully, Nick had taken his revolver with him to

Montana, and he put the deer out of its misery. We hiked into the dude ranch to call Gran and Gramps for a ride the rest of the way home. Our car was demolished, and I later bought a yellow Falcon wagon that would last us the next few years.

I had another sad animal incident commuting to and from school along Military Road, right at the division of a Y in the road with a 7-Eleven on the west side while lower on the east branch was a row of houses. A large black lab bounded down the hill from the store on my right and smashed into my car. I stopped in the parking area and went back. There, with the dog, was a boy about nine years old, much shaken, but able to get home with his dog under his own power. I asked the boy if he wanted me to go with him or take them to a vet. He said no and headed to one of the houses.

I kept thinking about that beautiful animal during dinner and as soon as I finished, I went back to the boy's house and knocked on the door. When I asked, I found out that his folks had not been home when the dog had been hit, and it had died. I was so sorry I had not packed the boy and dog up and taken them to my vet. I guess that would not have been kosher—and the boy *had* refused. Sometimes there is nothing you can do. I still wish I had been more directive and had insisted on some action. I do not like standing back and not knowing what to do; I always admire those who step in with authority to take charge.

That area was similar to another place along Military Road where I had a frightening experience not too long after that. I was driving home from work, and a little girl who was probably four years old broke away from her mother's grasp and ran almost into the road right in front of my car. At the last minute, she turned around and ran back. I pulled into a store parking lot and just sat there, shaking. If she had not changed directions, I would not have been able to stop the car and would have hit her.

Yes, all of life seems fraught with uncertainties and chance happenings of the there-but-for-the-grace-of-God variety. Thank you, God. My "luck of the draw" had struck once again.

20

DIFFERENT HAPPENINGS

*A*big change came into our lives in the summer of 1969. A good friend who was also a teacher called and said, "Waitresses are on strike. Why don't we give it a try?" The kids weren't eager for me to do it until I said they could have my tips. I tried the new endeavor. Well, it was not new because, during high school, I had walked through the power plant and crossed the suspension bridge over Snoqualmie Falls to wait tables at the Snoqualmie Falls Lodge. But this time, I gave waiting in the bar a try. I was not good there as I was unfamiliar with most of the drinks, was not into brand labels, and found that regular customers expected you to know their drink of choice when they sat down. No memory. Couldn't do that.

However, I did meet and start going with my next husband, a tugboat-seafaring man who was out to sea and then in. Two years later after a stretch on the East Coast, he called and asked me to meet him at the airport. Just as I received the call, I saw my latest purchase being delivered down the driveway. My son and I had looked around for recreational vehicles and found a turquoise 1947 International school bus that had been converted into an RV. When I picked Bob up at the airport, he asked me to marry him.

The 1947 International school bus that we converted into an RV.

My new seafaring husband bought a donkey for backpacking trips with his hiking buddy. He cemented a large pole at the back of the garage to help lift the box he had rigged to transport the donkey into his truck. Using my sewing machine, he made saddle bags. The donkey brayed loudly whenever someone came to the house, prompting one of Chuck's friends to declare, "That's quite a doorbell you have."

One Christmas, we decided to surprise our hiking buddies. I put a scarf over my head and shoulders, wrapped a doll in a blanket, climbed on the donkey, and Bob led me down the neighbor's drive-way, through backwoods, past the water tower, and to the backpacking buddy's house—the equivalent of about three blocks. They were indeed surprised and said, "Hello, Mary and Joseph, won't you come in for a drink? Leave the donkey outside."

Years earlier, I had enjoyed several trips with Gran and Gramp's horse groups in the mountains. When Chuck was about two, he was included on a weekend trip to a dude ranch with us. Growing up, the kids had horses. One day Laurie's horse was tied to the porch while I

Pedro, our doorbell, getting ready for a backpacking trip.

Gramp on an outing with Laurie and Chuck on horses.

was standing there visiting, and Val reached over and nipped me in the boob. I was not pleased. Later, when she was tied to the same post, she pulled away, toppling the porch. Another time, she got tangled in a rope and not only needed a visit from the vet, but I also had the job of giving her shots for a week to prevent infection. Much later, I would delight in a weeklong horse camp with my daughter and grandchildren. Horses would play a large part in my daughter's life; for years she has had three of them on her nine acres and just recently built a commendable corral to work with them.

I have had some disappointing experiences involving horses. My first memory of a horse was very strange, and it was possibly my first sex education as well. When I was kindergarten age, I was riding home on the back of a neighbor boy's bike. We rode past a male horse "taking a piss," as he put it, or as my mother would correct, "urinating." Bobby asked me how I would refer to the appendage in use at the moment.

Chuck's horse Chester with Duchess,
the dog that my children's dad, Fritz, had given them.

Having no brother yet, I was completely ignorant of such things, and he proceeded, for what seemed like an hour, to spout out words I had never heard. He was obviously proud of his male eloquence.

A couple of years later, I was thrown off a horse. My sister, a family friend, and I were sitting on a horse as my father, unfamiliar with such a chore, was holding the reins. The horse bucked us off and headed for the barn. My sister was knocked out while I landed in a mud puddle, requiring another shampoo. Still later, I was riding a friend's horse. Maybe I should say I was sitting on it when it started to run. I am not a very commanding person; I couldn't make it stop. A closed gate was ahead of us, and I was sure he would sail over it with me likely to fly through the air. Thankfully, he stopped at the gate, and I stayed seated.

But the thing I feel worst about is that Chuck's horse Chester began to go downhill before we noticed, and I blame myself for not keeping

My husband Bob gardening.

a better eye on things. I have said I believed in independence but when I look back later, I realize there was a share of neglect mixed in also, since at times I seemed to be more into my own activities than motherhood. The men in my life enjoyed nightlife, social times, outdoor backpacking, river rafting, and boating, and I was right in there with them. Years later, I happened to mention to my son that I did too much drinking when he was younger. Always thoughtful, he replied, "It wasn't apparent."

Always enjoying a play on words, I picked up on one he hadn't intended. I noticed and replied, "That was the effect. Not 'the parent' I should have been." Another one of those "I should have known better." Oh, why didn't I know better? Think ahead? And act better?

Backpacking at Dead Man's Lake.

21

THE HERO WHO SAVED THE DAY

I always thought I handled big things well. When enough small things add up, I have a great deal of difficulty keeping my cool, but usually, when a big thing comes around, I just knuckle under and clamp down on my reactions so I can figure out what to do. I found that not to be the case in the fall of 1971 when my son was fourteen years old. That summer, the seagoing man I had married was out for three months. He had decreed, "There is only one captain to a ship." Of course, that was him at home also.

I have often been disgusted with myself when realizing, after the fact, *that* I have—and the *extent* to which I have—gone along with someone else's plan for how things will be. Upon arriving on *our* scene, Bob declared that our two dogs (always free before to come and go inside or out) were to be kept outside. He bought a doghouse, placed it against the back of the house, and took off on his tugboat.

On my own when I bought the house in the spring of 1966, I had settled in with a boy and a girl and no third bedroom. The kids each took a bedroom, while I put a bed in a utility area beside the kitchen for me. The summer after we were married, Bob built the garage into a large, spacious bedroom-sitting room for us and joined it to the house by closing in the back porch. But at this time, there was still a back door that opened onto a concrete-slab back porch. The back door had a window that played an important role in the happenings of this night. The doghouse was past that by about six feet and butted up against the window to my son's bedroom.

At the time, we had our second little black poodle, Peppy, a rambunctious son of Kookla. We also had the dear and gentle German shepherd-coyote named Duchess, recently inherited. My current husband was on his way to Borneo on his tugboat.

After finishing my sewing project late one night, I settled into bed in the utility area. I did not fall asleep as my head hit the pillow; rather, I busily planned my activities for the next day. In this hazy state, bright flashes seeped through my closed eyelids. It took a while for my brain to register this unusual and puzzling phenomena, but finally I opened my eyes to see changing red and orange colors and shapes dancing through the window. I watched this visual display before deciding this was not for my entertainment but an unusual occurrence that I should question. *What is going on now?* I got out of bed and went to the window. *Oh, my God. The doghouse is on fire.*

I quickly turned to a table beside the back door and reached for the phone. The phone was there, *but where were the emergency numbers? I just reorganized them yesterday. But where?* I had gone through one of my organizational spells, putting every bit of information in order. I had it all ... but ... *where did I put them?* My mind kept turning over and over. I still don't know how I can completely quit thinking during times of stress. Quit seeing what is right in front of me. Sometimes quit seeing what is right in my hand. I gave up on finding the telephone numbers.

This was before the 911 emergency number existed. If it had, I wonder now if I would have managed to think to dial it, and if not, what number would I have called?

Okay, Plan B—water, a hose. I tried to think. *But the hose is not hooked up to the back faucet ... and it would take too long to go out to the shed and get another one to hook up. A hose is hooked up to the front faucet, but it won't reach around the house this far.*

Well then, Plan C—I can smother it. I went to my son's bedroom where extra blankets were stored in his closet. The door opened into his room with the bed across the space to the closet. Expedience trumped delicacy, thankfully, and I stepped up onto his bed and over him to get to the closet. In the process, I woke my son. That was the smartest thing I did that night.

Sitting up in bed, he asked, "What do you want?"

I said, "The doghouse is on fire. I need to put it out." I blurted that I couldn't find the emergency numbers to call the fire department. I told him that the only hose hooked up was to the front faucet. I added that I was going to try to smother the fire with a blanket.

The burned doghouse.

Chuck called out the telephone number of the fire chief, who happened to be the father of his best friend, and he headed to the front of the house. He went through the door, leaving it open. I thought, *What a strange time to leave, and where is he going?* Then I saw him pulling the hose through the living room, past the dining room table, and out the back door. He went back into the house to turn on the water and, as he came through, despite his very manly actions during this emergency, it was apparent he was still part young boy. In a soft, vulnerable voice, he said, "Mom, I don't know if I want to put this fire out."

I asked, "Why not?"

He aimed the stream of water from the hose at the blazing doghouse and said, "I'm afraid of what's inside."

Gently I said, "Chuck, turn around." When he did, he saw, standing over to the side, his two beloved pets. They were watching him be the hero of the day with expressions worn only by dogs.

When the fire was completely out and the hose was back in the front yard, we sat down in the kitchen. I said, "I don't know how that could have happened. Whatever would have started a fire there?"

Chuck hemmed and hawed, wondering if he could get around the answer. He dropped his eyes, and in a sheepish voice, he told me why it had happened. He felt sorry for the dogs outside in the cold. He knew he was not to let them in, so he'd found a solution to make them comfortable. It was an electric blanket from the closet plugged into the outlet in his room. Opening the window, he had dropped the blanket out and closed the window down to the cord. Then he had put the blanket in the doghouse, doubling it over to fit. He said he didn't think I would care, since I don't like electric blankets anyway.

Tragedy had been averted. We talked about the difference between my caring about what was done with an electric blanket and the safety factor in the correct use of one. I gave him the only reasons we still had an intact house over our heads:

1. I am a night owl and had gone to bed late.
2. There is a window in the back door.
3. The doghouse was sitting on a concrete slab, not a wooden deck or porch.
4. The siding on the house was not wooden but asbestos.
5. The fifth and most important reason: I have a very cool-headed and smart young son.

I added, "Oh yes, the dogs will be coming inside."

22

PRODUCE, HUTCHES, AND COOPS

For a few years, we tried our hands at farming—on a small scale, of course. I was used to this from my childhood. My father had dug a large vegetable garden by each of the five houses I lived in while growing up, and my mother's family were dairy farmers in Wisconsin and then fruit ranchers when they settled in Sunnyside, Washington. So, I thought nothing of it in 1973 when Bob plowed up the whole side pasture, plus most of the front one, and planted a huge garden. We had everything from garlic and potatoes, including Yukon Gold, to several rows of raspberries and asparagus. He planted a few fruit trees as well. This was, of course, in addition to all the usual peas, beans, carrots, onions, chard, lettuce, corn, squash, broccoli, cauliflower, beets, tomatoes, and so forth. I had not gotten into outdoor living yet, and I admit that he did most of the work of growing. My turn came at the time of harvest, when I picked, cleaned, canned, froze, jammed, packaged, stored, or cooked my way through the prolific produce.

Because of the garden, we already had a freezer when Bob decided to raise rabbits. He built hutches in the back, brought in two of those critters, and the process began. As a child, I remembered eating rabbit meat given to us by our neighbors, who had hutches in their backyard. I do not remember whether I enjoyed rabbit at that time, but I was soon to find out that I didn't like their meat at all this time. My favorite part was missing—the skin—and besides, I thought the meat was stringy. It wasn't at all as tasty to my way of thinking as chicken was. I didn't mind cutting up or cooking the rabbit—I just didn't like eating it. Somehow the rabbits and their hutches just seemed to disappear, but their pelts stayed around longer.

Being a craftsperson and frugal as well, I used whatever was at hand. Not too long before this time, I had bought an old fur coat at a thrift shop and used it to trim the flared hem of a black wool dress I had sewn. I then made a fur muff to go with it. They looked really sharp, so I decided to make good use of the beautiful rabbit fur. Waiting for the time and expertise I would need to tan the hides, I wrapped them well in plastic and stored them in the freezer.

My first husband Fritz was a holdover from the early mountain men, and soon after we divorced, he moved to a family farm in Montana to live off the land. During the time we were still married and living in the Snoqualmie Valley, he had a shed with pelts from a variety of animals he trapped. When I went grocery shopping, he might go along to pick out turnips and parsnips to be used for his trapping. Magazines advertising the necessities for trapping and hunting would lie around the house, and packages of all sorts of animal scents arrived in the mail. I was smart enough to aim my nose in the opposite direction and not pursue my curiosity there. In the shed hung metal traps of different sizes and configurations, as well as flat boards with rounded ends to stretch the skins after he removed the innards—I do not know what he did with those.

I remember a time when he and his friend poached a deer, and we spent the night at the friend's house playing poker with my son's piggy bank money. This was while the deer was hanging outside from a tree to bleed out. Chuck slept through the night on the couch, none the wiser that we were playing free and loose with his future savings. We did not get tracked down by the warden, and the next day the deer was cut up and packaged to go to the meat locker.

Sometime later, I looked up the directions for tanning a rabbit hide: "Soak and rinse hides in cold water. Do not stretch or dry. Squeeze out excess water and dry with a cloth. Remove all fat. Hides can be put on a stretcher to remove fat if this makes it easier for you. Don't remove the layers of membrane, just the fat. Slit the pelt down the belly and legs, so it lies flat. Mix together two parts salt, one part saltpeter, and two parts powdered alum. Measure parts by volume, not weight. Saltpeter and alum can be purchased at the drugstore. Sprinkle on the skin and rub in well. Roll up the skin starting at the head end. Roll individually in several layers of newspaper to absorb the excess water. Place in a plastic bag and fasten with a twist tie. Keep in a cool place for fourteen (14) days."

I read through to the end of the recipe for the chore I had planned on tackling. Instead, I went out to the freezer to get the hides, grabbed a shovel, and headed to the far reaches of our land to dig a hole and bury them. I threw the plastic bag in the garbage can. Other crafts beckoned to me more—those less smelly and time-consuming.

Before this time, while we still had rabbits and all the flavor of the farm around us, I decided I would do my part and raise chickens. We could have our own eggs. I got the idea at the local feed store when picking up food for the rabbits and the donkey. There I saw a small pen with baby chickens hatching out of beautifully colored eggs. I learned that these chickens, called Araucanas, were originally raised by the indigenous people of South America. The hens had different colors, markings, and patterns and laid eggs in shades of blue, green, gold, and pink—some were brightly colored while others were pale or dull. I learned the color of the hen did not determine the color of the egg, although an individual hen always laid the same color of egg.

I was so thrilled with this display and thought, *Oh, how wonderful. And what fun.* Bob could raise his rabbits and I could raise my chickens. I know, I know. Anyone hearing this who grew up on a farm would cock their ears, raise their eyebrows, and comment, "Is she crazy or what?" They would know ahead of time the actualities involved. Those meant getting up even earlier in the morning than I already did—even when the weather was cold, wet, and miserable. Not only getting up but also putting clothes on to go outside to feed and water the critters, even though I would have to come back in and change clothes to get ready for school. Did I mention—I hate to get up early? Did I mention—I hate to change clothes? Did I think of the fact that cats and dogs are a very different matter? They are fed indoors. Keeping water for them is an easy matter. If I forget to give them water, they can go down to the pond.

And they always have a constant water supply—the toilet. My animals have usually lived very long lives, despite my smoking in the house for many years, so I do not believe that they have been neglected or abused by drinking from that built-in water trough.

I know I have often been naïve. I tend to go into things with grand, eager plans, and Bob was willing to encourage me in my endeavors. He took his truck down to Mossy Rock and returned with a chicken coop. I wish I had a picture of that—a yellow Nissan pickup truck with an old, weather-beaten, very used-looking building tied on the back, looking like it would fall off at any moment. Then he backed up his truck to the east side of the garage. I use that term "garage" loosely. When I bought the house, an old building stood behind it that had been used as a broom factory. I don't know if that endeavor was the previous owner's vocation or avocation, but the bare boards of the walls were covered with black Visqueen plastic affixed with nailed-on broom handles. While gardening, I found the dirt to be green from the commonly used green dye used with brooms at the time. Bob had installed a pull-up garage door and used this shed as a garage. It was behind this building that he deposited my chicken coop, waiting for fencing to be installed.

One evening, we went on the motorcycle to dinner with another teacher at my school. We enjoyed a few drinks, a good dinner, and a lot of visiting. We saw the house projects they were working on and her husband's recent art. We came home as we had left, with me on the back of the motorcycle. But instead of turning in at our driveway, Mr. Steve McQueen turned at the fire station and down into the field across from our house. After tooling around the soccer field, he headed up the hill to our street. This hill was about a yard high with an approximately fifty-degree grade, maybe a little steeper. Bob did this often. However, with the added weight of another person, the motorcycle gave out and tipped over.

It wasn't a bad spill except for the freakishness of breaking both bones in my left ankle as I landed. Knowing Bob underplays anything physical, I did not want him to grab my foot and say "Oh, there's nothing wrong with this," so I whined and said, "This is bad." Then instead of staying where I was for him to bring the car to me, I made a big mistake of crawling up the hill to meet him at the road. This meant mucho tissue damage, two surgeries, a cast up to my thigh, and crutches for months. By the time I was healed enough to even look behind the garage, the coop was gone. I was saved from chickens.

23

LOOKING OVER MY SHOULDER
WHILE WALKING AHEAD

*A*t the end of what I called the "Early Years" era, I looked back at the roads traveled.

Along with my graduation from high school, marriage, and the birth of my children, the 1950s brought inflation, the building of bomb shelters, McCarthy, an average annual income of $4,000, gasoline at twenty cents a gallon, my first house with ten acres for $10,000, and rock 'n' roll.

In the 1960s, after divorce, graduation from college, and my first teaching job, and while my children were young, I traipsed across the country with a Coast Guard lieutenant during the times of the Cuban missile crisis and the Bay of Pigs, President Kennedy, the Cold War, an Apollo test launch, Russia's first soft-moon landing, civil rights, Martin Luther King, demonstrations, and the Vietnam War.

At the end of 1969 and through the 1970s, along with miniskirts and bell-bottoms and while my children were growing up, I was into a second marriage, during which we made trips in a remade 1947 International school bus, water-skied on the Columbia River at Vantage, hiked, backpacked, river-rafted, sailed in our sailboat, and flew in my husband's Cessna while the world experienced the space race, a man landed on the moon, hippies and flower power grew, and men sprouted more hair. The smiley face symbol first appeared in Seattle, and the Beatles and the Rolling Stones arrived on the scene. We pulled out of Vietnam, headed into the sexual revolution with more women's rights, and watched *All in the Family* and *Happy Days*.

From the late 1970s into the 1980s, the digital revolution started, along with the beginning of the home computer, video games, microwave ovens, email, and the barcode, while Boeing 747 air travel boomed, causing new problems with pollution.

Laurie enjoying an equine outing with her beloved Gran.

Yes, the years went by, my children grew up, and more animals moved through our lives with love, joy, frustration, pain, and loss. It was a busy time. Through all these years, we had the wonder of births with Tiger, Kookla, and Duchess, and we once counted eighty guppies popping out on Father's Day. There were mild frustrations, including a missing Duchess, but great elation when I picked her up at the pound. We experienced anxieties with sicknesses like what Sparky and Sasha suffered, shots for Val, and all the caregiving that animals require. Many difficult decisions were made, like leaving Sparky and an undeveloped kitten behind at the vet's office. There were tragedies with the demise of our beloved pets Kookla, Sasha, and Duchess. There was Peppy, who wandered away when it seemed a "good day to die."

I cringed, remembering situations where I had failed creatures and children by not being more attentive, such as when a couple of animals were rescued from tangled ropes, a horse barely survived a low supply of water, and a door opened to inadvertently release Kookla into the street in the path of a passing car. I figured that in the next period of my life, there would be more joys with animals, along with births, disappointments, and losses—all a part of life with pets. All a part of life.

As I thought of these animals winding their way in and out of my life during those early times, I found myself also thinking back to the three men who, like the animals, seemed to have wandered in and then out. What life lessons was I missing to have made the choices I did— and causing relationships to not work?

Years later, I would learn about unresolved childhood issues and about being too defensive to build a good relationship. I would learn that when you have those leftover issues, you tend to choose someone with similar wounds so both partners automatically activate the other person's old behavior patterns.

Later, for the first time, it would occur to me to consider the effects on my children of the choices I made. I had come this far in my life as if on automatic pilot, taking care of the necessities—and my wants— without giving thought to the fine-tuning needed to prepare my children for a better future. But consideration of this was yet to come. I was still looking backward after the fact. It hadn't yet occurred to me to look down the road to the other end, consider the bumps ahead, and find a way to make better decisions for the morrow.

That little duck at the beginning of my story set out like I did, disregarding the advice of her elders to do what she wanted. I wonder if she learned to make better choices. Did she look back and consider what led to her unwise choices so she could do better in the future? I would never know about that little duckling, but I would eventually start to learn about those things for myself.

Part II

Asking Questions

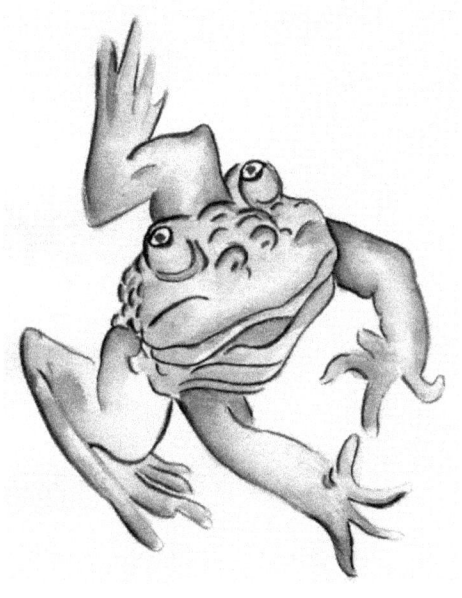

Looking forward to working in my world.

A FROG PROLOGUE

The week had been long and tiring. Turning the windshield wipers on at high speed, I drove home over patches of greenery strewn across the road from powerful winds. Where did this carpet of green come from? For the first time, I noticed old, tired, used-up trees at the sides of the road leaning not only over the road but also over the power lines. *No wonder we have so many power outages*, I thought. I pulled into my driveway to discover cedar and fir confetti covering the whole 150 feet. Driving over the small, downed branches, I uttered my wish: *Oh, please, no loss of power tonight.*

Inside, I dropped the week's art projects and my grade book onto the dining table, kicked off my shoes, and headed to the back of the house. I was looking forward to changing my clothes and settling in for the weekend.

That familiar feeling of something not quite right crept into my awareness. My feet felt creepy. And cold. And wet? The sensation soaked through my socks to attack my feet. It was then that I noticed a large dark circle on the floor. I kept watching it grow larger and larger, and the message finally traveled to my brain—leakage. I immediately looked up at the ceiling, fearful of a rush of water from overhead.

Noticing nothing out of order there, I pulled my eyes back down to roam around the room. Antique secretary, big oak desk, built-in bookshelves, couch, fish tank, chest ... all okay. With a puzzled shake of my head, I stopped surveying and jerked my gaze back to the fish tank. The water line was down to less than three inches, with fish crowded together, looking out in distress. The floor was definitely distressed. I made a distressed threesome as I realized the direction of my weekend.

After changing into grubby clothes, I moved fish, frogs, and snails into the smaller two-by-three-foot fish tank situated just past the large and now defunct hexagonal one standing on the floor. A neon tetra pushed his nose up to the edge, gave me a baleful look while treading water in his formerly cushy home, and pleaded with me, *What is happening? I liked the way things were. Why do they have to change?*

I paused to return his look. *Yeah, I know. I'm sorry this happened, too. But you know, Tetsi, nothing stays the same. Changes occur. Losses of one sort or another continue to disrupt our lives. Nothing to do but get used to it, so buck up, little guy, and hang in there while I move you to your new home.* I added, *Just be grateful you aren't the one who has to clean up this mess.* I swooped him up into my net and released him into the smaller but still operable tank.

While moving more fish from the broken tank, I thought of when I started the fish tanks nearly twenty years earlier. As I released more frantic residents from the diminishing water, I thought about *my* current tank, housing me for thirty years. I had bought the house in March 1966. My first child and first grandchild were born in March. And the frogs in the pond always arrive then. Year after year, I eagerly await what I call the "waking of the frogs," a raucous chorus of thousands of little green and brown tree frogs singing their hearts out in my back acreage.

Reminded of frogs, I started hunting for my African dwarf frogs. They were hiding in the plant life, of course. I captured Olive Oil and Sienna and lifted these two wriggling masses of fear into the full tank of water. I had to search for several minutes until I found Umber down at the bottom in a pile of caved-in foliage. He joined his brothers with great glee. I stood and watched them for some time as they jumped around with joy at having enough water again to do what they do best.

Transferring the rest of the floundering fish, I thought back on the time that later ushered in what I refer to as the "Middle Years." As so often happens, several changes had occurred within a short time.

When my children were younger, there was always activity. My kids, their friends, and my friends were in and out of the house in what seemed like a constant flurry of activity, and, of course, accompanied by an assortment of animals. As the children grew and became more independent, my social director husband and I kept busy with family and friends, some travel, and many sporting activities: backpacking, river rafting, sailing, snowshoeing, ice skating, fishing, motorcycling, and flying.

After my children finished school and left home, the last of the "Early Years" animals passed away, and my husband, a wonderful man interested in taking on any new learning or activity, wanted to build a small house in his hometown and spend large parts of the year in Mexico, Arizona, and Alaska. I am a dedicated homebody, loving the home I already have, and I did not want to move. I don't like to travel either, so we divorced but continued to see each other with deep regard for several years until he remarried.

After the divorce, my way of life changed completely. I lived here alone and on my own for the next twenty years with a new contingent of pets and animals while I remodeled my house, added a second floor, built a studio, and landscaped my two acres. I nodded to the little swordfish I was moving: *Yeah, changes and disruptions happen to all of us. It's a way of life.*

I watched the frogs and thought, *Everything in the world passes through its stages. All is filled with beginnings, middles, and endings.* I once read that frogs are a missing link in evolution. I love patterns and cycles: the progression of evolution; the connection between water, land, and sky; and the interconnection between all of God's creatures and creations. A mother frog lays clumps of floating eggs in the weeds along the shallow edge of my pond in the springtime. These little round transparent bubbles the size of a pea or larger are connected in a chainlike fashion, becoming tadpoles or polliwogs. They have gills and squiggly tails until they approach the adult stage, when their legs and lungs develop, and their tails gradually disappear. All is progression, and we are all part of it.

Back to the present. Setting my reverie aside, I made sure no fish, frogs, or snails remained in the broken tank. I found a five-gallon pail in the shed and a pan with a handle in the kitchen. I pulled the plant life out and added it to the compost pile before removing the rocks and gravel. Bailing the rest of the water out of the tank, I trekked back and forth thirty feet to the bathroom to dump pails of water into the tub.

While I washed and dried the fish tank, I entertained myself with more thoughts. Problems of one manner or another kept coming along with messes to be cleaned up afterward. And … always there were decisions to be made. I wondered, *Had I learned to make better choices during my Middle Years than in the Early Ones?* Earlier, it seldom, if ever, occurred to me to think through the consequences of my actions before taking those actions—I just acted.

And looking back now, it seemed I was oblivious—and gave no thought to the morrow. I thought only later about what had happened by looking backward with the words, *Why didn't I know better? I should have known better.* If it occurred to me to think through the consequences, I probably would have pulled a Scarlett O'Hara: *Oh, I'll think about that tomorrow.* Or I would have looked for still another Rhett Butler to give direction to my life.

Pail in hand, I stopped to consider: *What about those questions not asked during my youthful years? And, more importantly, did I learn to ask them in my Middle Years? Did I learn to give more thought to the consequences of my actions? Did I think through the endings from the beginnings?*

I finished emptying and cleaning the fish tank and came back to the present. Time for a well-deserved Friday evening break. I sat sipping my glass of wine and looked around the room … and at the wet floor. What next? Well, as always, I will just have to find out as I live it.

24

CAGES, TANKS, AND PLANTS

*D*uring those Middle Years, I traded in couples' and sporting activities for more individual and creative ones. I published home economics educational materials, developed an art curriculum, and sold some art before starting the process of remodeling my house. While I worked on my projects, I listened to the radio, where I discovered Jennifer James and soaked up her advice for life skills I had missed.

Jennifer, a cultural anthropologist and a professor at the University of Washington School of Medicine, was the Billboard Personality of the Year in 1980, having started one of the first talk radio programs in the Northwest. Her program on KVI Radio in Seattle became number one, and in 1981, she began writing a column for *The Seattle Times* that was a top-rated feature for eighteen years. She then did television commentary for seven years and expanded her lecture business around the world. I soaked up her advice while I glued, hammered, spackled, sewed, and painted.

She told of her house with fish tanks and an aviary. The aviary I was not able or willing to do, but I managed a bird cage with a couple of parakeets for a while until I realized I was just being a copycat. I don't really want birds in my house anyway.

The fish were a different matter. For many years, I enjoyed a rectangular table tank and then added a larger hexagonal one on the floor, with frogs thrown into the mix. For the first time, I bought houseplants and sweet-talked them to a swift death. I bought a second bunch and spoke sharply to them, telling them to thrive or join the others in the compost heap. They lasted and flourished, perhaps because I added a small amount of neglect.

I enjoyed playing house on the weekends, taking care of birds, fish, and plants as well as cleaning and decorating. And I enjoyed remodeling my house on vacations and evenings. I enjoyed it all the more because it was all in my own time, my own space, and my own way. And, as I worked, I listened to new information that helped me fill in missing parts of my life.

I was the same me, I had the same job, and it was the same house. But oh, what a different life I had. Gradually, over the next several years, it became a different house, also. Alone for the first time ever, I took a different interest in my home. I had no fear of criticism or objection, and no one else's thoughts or opinions infringed upon me. Without the need, for the first time in my life, to consider another person's wants and equipped with unlimited time, I started knowing what I wanted to do and made the decision to change my world.

Along with the demise of the sports activities themselves went the need for their requisite equipment. Some of it was easy for me to get rid of, and others were harder. I hung onto my backpack for several years before finally leaving it at the Goodwill for someone else to enjoy. The smaller equipment—the golf clubs, baseball bats, croquet set, and basketball hoop, plus an assortment of balls of all sizes, shapes, and purposes, and the badminton rackets, nets, and poles—I stored in the garden shed for many years. It wasn't until years later, when I realized my grandchildren were never going to want any of it, that I piled it all into the car and headed back to Goodwill. Of course, I kept my tennis racket and still have my sleeping bag, hiking boots, and parka. And I did keep two putters, along with a bag of balls, thinking someday I would make a green on the pasture, and it was into the next century when my twin teenage great-granddaughters sunk two cans and tried putting the golf balls into them.

There was no longer a need for space to store the backpacks, sleeping bags, rubber rafts, air mattresses, tent, and outdoor cooking gear. Getting rid of this equipment allowed me to tear out the huge storage shelves housing them and make room for a large new window. Now outdoor light and scenery came pouring into this area that became my office. As I work at my computer on a desk made from a discarded closet door, I watch the neighbor's dogs and see the family of crows swoop down to their porch for the dog food left there. I roll my old oak chair around to the big solid oak desk bought for $47 at an auction on Pacific Highway back in 1974. Then, with my back to the window,

I face the "back room" where I can watch the antics of cats at play or catch a TV show as I work on boring chores like bills.

This back room was made when the wall of my son's bedroom was torn out, and the area of porch between the utility room and garage was added to form a T. Through the stages of this remodeling, my ex-husband had put up three different kinds of plastic paneling without consulting me. On my own now, I thought of Mexican restaurant walls, and, for the first time, I knew what the solution to this visual horror would be. Armed with pails and pails of Beadex All Purpose Premixed Joint Compound, I spackled all the walls of that area. I did not know if this compound would just slide off the slippery vinyl, but it didn't. It stayed up. And I painted over all the vinyl. Now, all three sections look like they actually belong together. And I was a happy camper—even though I was no longer up in the mountains near Mount St. Helen's at Deadman's Lake with a great companion, but nevertheless I was a happy camper in my own home.

I also gave up a small living-room closet to enlarge my bathroom. I bought packages of foot-square mirrors and glued them to the walls above the counters on the three-sided walls I now had. I could see my hair from three directions at a glance.

Through the years, I changed out every small, old wooden-framed window in the house for larger ones so I could look out at the nature surrounding me and bring the outside in to lighten my world. I brightened it even more with a couple of skylights. But even more important was tearing out the upper cupboards on the side of the kitchen that faced the back pasture and the pond. I then put big windows in what had been the utility room—now a dining room, albeit a small one. I installed sliding glass doors on that same back wall and built a deck across the back of the house, complete with an arbor to hold a wisteria vine. I even bought curved concrete blocks, built a barbecue on a corner of the deck, and later added a hot tub.

Now, with large windows on every side and the whole back of my house open to the woods, pasture, and pond, I started getting involved in the outside world as well. One summer as I was up on a ladder painting the exterior of the house, I paused to look at the job I was doing and thought of an expression my father used: "You can't make a silk purse out of a sow's ear." I pondered a bit and thought, *No, there is no way that this house could ever be a silk purse, no matter what I do. Ah, but it sure is a better sow's ear.* I painted a board and nailed it onto the cherry tree at the side of the driveway. It announced "a better" in small red letters above the larger black letters of "Sow's Ear," and it remained there for several years until it became too weather-worn to leave in place.

My wise, wonderful mother-in-law Gran in all her irrepressible spirit.

25

INTO EVERYONE'S HEART

*V*ery little in life seems to be all black or white, except for a number of my cats. Stages of life are not abrupt either, and the period ushering in this middle time blended back and forth for a few years. My ex-husband Bob and I remained in a relationship for about six years, and we continued taking trips on the sailboat (now his), trolling for fish off La Push on the fishing boat he refurbished in my driveway. Once, we even flew in his Cessna up for dinner at Rosario Resort for my birthday. In October of 1980, I learned at school about the rampage of the Fife Rapist and his brutal damage to women. I came home and found Bob sitting on the hearth ledge in the living room. He asked if I would like him to move in until the rapist was caught. I certainly would. He is such a wonderful man, and I was truly grateful.

My children also went through stages of going out into the world and coming back home for spells. My daughter lived in the area for a while and then went to work as a deckhand or a cook on fishing and crabbing boats in Alaska. Between seasons, she would stay here.

Off on one of her trips, Laurie left a pickup truck parked on the side of my carport. When pruning back the bamboo, I investigated the bed of the truck and saw a huge wooden burl lying in several inches of water. I rescued that lovely natural sculpture and brought it in to dry. I am sure the wood-knowledgeable men in my family have told me what kind of wood it is, but I do not remember. More important to me are the shapes, textures, and values. This sculpture is eighteen inches high and twenty-seven inches wide with a flat bottom, so it sits nicely on the ledge of my fireplace wall. Around the edge is a three-inch section of lighter color combined with wonderful darker swirls, while the interior cross-section is ridged as if cut with a rough saw. I always find God to be the best artist and enjoy many of His or Her pieces from nature.

Several years later, finished with her crabbing and fishing in Alaska, Laurie bought forty acres in Tonasket and asked for the burl back. It would have rotted and been ruined had I not rescued it from a watery grave. Thinking of squatter's rights, I selfishly said, "No." It is still on display on my living room mantel along with a beautiful fungus.

Before leaving for her seven years of adventures in Alaska, Laurie had acquired a dog, and in 1977, I was bequeathed this beautiful golden retriever-collie mixture named Jude. She was a delightfully gentle, calm soul who was to be with me for more than fifteen years. In those early days, there was little traffic on the street in front of our house, and life was still rural.

A girl down the road delivered the neighborhood's newspapers on her horse. Each afternoon, she stopped at the top of my driveway to pick up Jude, who eagerly trotted up to the road to join them on the trek around Fivemile Lake to deliver papers down long driveways to each house. This continued for a few years until the girl outgrew this job. One year, she returned from her vacation to gift me a colorful Mexican blanket. At that time, many horseback riders still passed along the road in front of my house. It has been painful for me to see the loss of that slow and natural life as the area becomes an increasingly busy suburb.

In the summer of 1978, I signed up for a week of river rafting in the Hells Canyon of the Snake River. This was to announce to myself I was able do things on my own without a social director, as I had labeled my older sister and ex-husband. I had been home for two days from this enjoyable solo adventure when Jude went missing in the evening. It was unusual for her to not come when I whistled, so I left the door open and went back to my book.

After a few pages, I saw a movement out of the corner of my eye, and Jude walked in the door. I was glad to see her. After giving her more attention, I saw a little bunch of fur hanging from her mouth. She came over to where I was on the couch, gently placed her precious gift on the floor at my feet, and looked up for my approval. This, of course, was freely given. After a short while, she picked up her baby and before

Jude nursing her ever-hungry puppies.

I could stop her, she went out the door and around to the side, where she was going to settle in underneath the house.

I did not know what I should do, but I took the pup from her and went back inside. I gathered towels and a box and put them in the utility room. After a while, Jude brought in another pup. This time I shut the door and showed her where to finish her deliveries. She soon settled down to the job of releasing the next six adorable bundles. She was a very good mommy and even appeared disheveled with all the work she gave to that job.

Three days later, the couple on the other side of the pond came to the door asking to see the puppies. Surprised, I asked, "How did you know?" They said they had seen Jude breed and had counted the time for the arrival. I was very impressed. Jude, as usual, had been very wise, having had her puppies early in November so they'd be adopted for Christmas and not left behind at the pound. A couple of days before Christmas, I sorrowfully scooped the babies into a box and took them to the pound. The lady assured me that because of the time of the year, they would all be adopted. I asked her how long they would be kept there if not claimed by loving families. After three days, I stopped back to roam the aisles and survey the cages. I was delighted to find that there were no little golden wonder dogs left, and I went home in peace,

Jude enjoying a belly rub from Laurie.

although years later, it occurred to me I certainly should have kept one of the pups. Another one of those wait-till-tomorrow moments to think of what I should have done yesterday.

When I was creating gardens at the front and back of the house, I brought up several boxes of river rocks from the river in the valley. After that, I found I often had to remove rocks from the lawn in order to mow it. I was puzzled. How did they get there? These weren't just little-bitty rocks, but good-sized hunks five or six inches in length. Then when I found a couple in the house, I began to question my sanity. Could I be a sleepwalker? A multiple personality? There was simply no one else around to do it.

One day while I was ironing, I caught the culprit in the act and solved the mystery. My jaw dropped open when I saw Jude sneaking in the door with a rock in her mouth. She looked up at me with that look of, "Uh-oh, she caught me." At that time, I had never heard of a stuffed toy for an animal; our animals always had live children, other animals, and the great outdoors for play. Since then, I have seen the neighbor's dogs wandering around their yard with stuffed toys hanging from their mouths. Poor Jude was a deprived pet. A rock is not at all cuddly, although to me, river rocks are lovely to look at.

Jude with Laurie and her daughter Shoshannah.

I told my son about the rocks, and he shared a similar story about his dog. Kona was a lovely German shepherd who lived across the street from a county park on Fivemile Lake. In the summer, a lot of traffic went by, so Chuck built a cyclone fence around his property. When someone walked by on the road, Kona would run along inside the entire thirty feet of fence on one side of the house, barking at the person. Then he would have to go around the back of the house and through a walkway between the house and the storage shed to catch up with and bark at that same person along the twenty feet on the other side of the house.

Kona had another habit. It didn't involve rocks, but he would carry a piece of wood in his mouth. Chuck had rebuilt his house from the bottom up, so several pieces of lumber were always lying around for a time. One day Kona was watching the neighborhood with a length of two-by-four in his mouth when someone came along the road. Kona went hell-bent around the house, planning to beat the walker to the other side. But the lumber was too long to fit through the space, and he came to an abrupt stop. Chuck said it looked like a slapstick comedy cartoon. I didn't ask how long his dog's mouth was sore.

One day in October of 1981, Jude did not come home. When she was still gone after three days, I went down to the animal shelter in Kent. I walked up and down the aisles, looking at all the dogs in the pens. Hoping, hoping, and thinking, *Maybe the next pen*. Then *Maybe down the next aisle*. My disappointment grew. And my fear. I wondered, *What do I do next? What more can I do?* I was so hoping she'd be there. When she wasn't, I was afraid I'd never see her again.

I asked the lady at the pound what their procedure was. Every three days, they disposed of any animal that was left, so I continued to trudge through the pound every three days looking into the faces of those eager ones pleading, *Please pick me*, or the broken-spirited ones emoting, *I don't really care anymore*. Still no luck. I continued for a couple more weeks; I didn't know how long was too long. I finally decided it was time to quit, and I reconciled myself to her being gone. I dreaded the thought of telling Laurie.

Then, when Jude had been gone for three weeks, I heard a noise at the door and found a very bedraggled, dirty, and matted Jude. Someone had to have picked her up and taken her. She was a very desirable and lovely dog not only in appearance but also in temperament as well. Anyone would want her, but I did not think much of their way of trying to get her. I was so glad she had pulled a Lassie move and returned home.

At one point when my daughter was once again settled in a home, she asked if she could have Jude back. Again, I told her no. Jude had been with me for so many years that I did not want to change her lifestyle, or mine either. We enjoyed many good years together, but inevitably she began to go downhill. I took her to the vet, and he advised that I might want to think about putting her to sleep.

On May 23, 1991, Jude gave me an imploring look. She could not get up. I went out to the back pasture and dug a hole. I lifted her into the back of the wagon and returned to the vet. I asked if he would give her the final injection in the car so I could take her home for burial on my acreage. I was surprised when he complied; I didn't think it was legal. After he gave her the shot, I drove her home and slid her into her final resting place beside a stump in the back pasture alongside Kookla, Duchess, and other beloved pets gone to their much-deserved rest.

Twenty years later, I lovingly lifted her leather collar from the hook where it had hung, and with tears, placed it in the garbage.

Yeah, Jude came into everyone's heart and made it better.

My garden and backyard.

A PAIR OF CALICOES

A couple of years after Laurie left Jude with me, I returned home from La Push after a disastrous trip on Bob's fishing boat. There had been a storm, the boat's engine had failed, and we had drifted through the night. Of course, during this whole time, my vivid Irish imagination conjured up the worst possible scenarios—drifting to the other side of the ocean, crashing into a ship, sinking, being pulled under by a giant octopus—yes, I do have an anxious nature as well as a vivid imagination. The next day, we were rescued and pulled to shore by those oceanic powers that exist to rescue terrified ex-wives from a watery grave. I finally and gratefully arrived home and drove down my driveway.

There, sitting by the front porch was a small calico cat. She looked up at me as if to say, "Well, here I am." The whole front of her body, sides, and legs were pure, fluffy white. From just in front of her ears over her head, down her back, and the length of her tail were large, distinct shapes of black and reddish orange. The reddish color also sat on her face in an unfortunate splotch. This gave her the look of a little kid with a perpetually dirty face. I played with the word *calico. Cali.* A catchy Hank Williams tune from the fifties came to mind, and I named her Kaw-Liga.

Oh great, that would be this little gal's name. Well, Kali now had her name, and she quickly made herself at home. She would prove to be the first of several calicoes to wander my way.

About a year later, at around noon on a Saturday, I pried and chipped a large slab of ugly old linoleum off the kitchen counter and threw it onto the growing pile of scraps on the table. I had hated this countertop since moving in over ten years earlier. As I worked, I thought, *Well, it's not as bad as the floor was.* I glanced down at my floor with a smug look. I loved the camouflage solution I had chosen to hide the horrible old linoleum relic—I had covered all the floors throughout the house with natural-fiber, woven raffia mats from Trident. Looking up, I smiled with delight at the matching raffia cloth I had used to paper the walls; its beige coloring gave a warm glow to the house.

Kaliga striking up her "Here I am" pose.

Then I looked over at the boxes of ceramic tile and pails of adhesive waiting on the other end of the table. I had chosen tiles on sale at ColorTile on my way home from school. Questions already niggled at my mind: *Will I still like this choice next week? Will I be able to do a decent job of installing them? How will they wear?* Then, in another tone of voice, I chided myself for always choosing the most economical supplies and at the first place I saw them. I argued back, *With the cheaper ones, I can do more projects, and choosing the closest store gives me more time.* I added *Always choices.* I kept chipping away at the linoleum as I entertained myself with the ongoing radio program inside my head.

Then I felt something brush against my leg and looked down. There was Kali, moving back and forth, making strange noises. She looked up at me with the imploring look of the truly distressed. I finished pulling away the chunk of linoleum I had just loosened with the chisel and bent down to ask what was troubling her. She had no chance to reply to my inquiry but dropped an enclosed mass of jelly onto the floor. Looking closer, I determined it to be several undeveloped kittens. *Oh no, I didn't even know she was pregnant.* As I cleaned it up, I thought,

What a shame, she would have been a good mommy. I abandoned my project for the afternoon and snuggled down on the couch with Kalija to console her for her loss.

Three years after Kali arrived, I walked over to the front window with my morning cup of coffee. A little ball of brown, rust, and white fur came down the driveway—a scraggly, dirty, disheveled, hungry, (and as I was to find out later) buggy kitten. She had obviously been dumped along the road, but she came down my driveway as if she knew exactly what she was doing and where she was going. And she kept coming right up to the door. When I opened it to let her in, I wondered if someone had marked my driveway—like they did during the Depression to let the hobos know where they could get a meal.

I had been playing records Laurie had left at the house, including five or six albums by Cat Stevens. I especially like the songs from his *Numbers* album. I immediately thought of the lyrics from "Jzero." And so, Jzero became her name.

Jzero was exotic-looking with a small head and larger-than-normal ears that stood straight up. She also had a white belly and the same colors on her back as Kali but in a smaller, mottled pattern and without the dirty marks on her face. Kalija had arrived first, and I loved them both, but for some reason, Jzero was the one who captured deeper heartstrings. She was independent but also more attached to me than any other animal had been. It was as if this were the first pet who was just mine, and I was very partial to her. After about a year, it became apparent she was going to become a mommy. I really hoped that she would be able to carry through with the chore and not abort as Kalija had done.

One morning, I could not find Jzero anywhere. I soon heard what sounded like mewing in the utility room. I looked around, but she was nowhere to be seen. I was sure I was hearing kittens and that she had had her babies, but I couldn't find them. I walked back and forth along the wall where I heard the noises. Finally, I lifted the trapdoor in the floor to access the cramped crawl space beneath the house. Shining a flashlight into that musty area, I still couldn't see them, but their noises were even louder.

An "a-ha" of what had happened finally sank in. When I remodeled the bathroom, I had found a space of more than a foot between the kitchen and bathroom walls. I now figured Jzero had crawled into an open vent at the side of the house and up into that space, and I could not reach her delivery room to retrieve the babies. I paced around, wondering what to do and afraid that if they stayed in total darkness too long, the little ones wouldn't be able to see. After fussing and fretting through the afternoon, I finally grabbed hammer and saw and broke through the end wall to cut out a section big enough to allow them to come out.

The pert, independent Jzero.

But my very independent Miss Jzero did not come out. She was quite settled in with her precious progeny, and I could not reach in far enough to pick them up. Shining the light, I looked inside. And I gasped. A slot had been built into an ancient medicine cabinet I had discarded when remodeling. For years the former owners had slid their used razor blades through the slot, which then fell onto the floor between the walls. And this was the very floor where my Jzero and her precious wee ones were wriggling around. I still could not reach in far enough to safely lift them out and away from the razor blades.

Jzero with two of her kittens.

Putting on my problem-solving hat, I wandered around the house until it worked its magic. I then went out to the shed for a piece of mat board, cut it to the width of the area between the walls and long enough to reach the kittens, slid it between the two walls, and dropped it down to the floor so it reached right up to the first nestled kitten. I brought the broom inside the house, inserted it into the space in the wall, swept that little baby onto the mat board, and lifted him out of the razor blades and to where I could pick him up. Then I pushed the board back in to coax the other kitty siblings to climb aboard and pulled them out. With the kittens safely out and ensconced in a cardboard bed lined with soft towels, of course Momma followed of her own accord.

Later, I found homes for four of the kittens and planned to keep two. One day I came home from school to find them gone. I thought it rather unlikely that someone had come down my long driveway to abscond with the kittens. The thought always niggled in the back of my mind: *Did Jzero have anything to do with the dirty deed of their disappearance?* Soon afterward, Kali took to periodically wandering off and then returning after a short period of time. I wondered if Jzero had acted like a mean older sister, telling her she wasn't wanted. Maybe Momma did not like competition. I never did find out where Kali went on her periodic walkabouts, but I was glad she always came back. Several neighborhood cats had disappeared from raccoons or opossums in the area. Thank goodness Kali escaped that fate.

27

FRUSTRATIONS:
FLIVERS, FLEAS, AND FIREPLACES

What is the total lifetime of messes spent in cleanup? I do entertain myself while I deal with the mundanities of life, like making up words to describe categories of types of messes. Anything for my mind to occupy itself while cleaning up after animals. There are, of course, the weekly chores of cleaning the fish tanks and the bird cage, washing the dog and cat dishes, and watering and sponging off the plants. These duties I enjoy on the weekends as I clean the house and change the decorations. But cleanup beyond those tasks often try my patience and rile me up.

There are times when effort I have not welcomed is foisted on me by the animals in my house. At two different times, critters have come down my fireplace. The first instance involved two little four-legged, furry somethings-or-others. I was startled one cold winter school morning by unusual noises as I hurried from the bathroom to the kitchen in search of coffee. I found the commotion in the fireplace.

I did not know what the culprits were or how vicious they might be without the protection of the glass fireplace doors. I did not know what to do, and I did not want to open the doors and let them loose into the house. And, I didn't really have the time to deal with them, or I would be late for school. So, I decided to just leave them where they were and take care of the dead bodies after they died; I could pick them up later and throw them out in the woods.

That was not very kind of me, but, at the moment, earning a living took precedence. This was shortly after I started my years of living by myself. I was still working, it was the dead of winter, and well—what can I say—I did not have many creative problem-solving juices flowing. But I was saved from guilt, because, when I got home from school, the mysterious creatures had somehow climbed back up the chimney and escaped from their temporary stopping place.

The next critter to appear in my fireplace was a bird. Since it was not a school day this time, I had plenty of time to think and plot my course of action. I wanted to set the bird free, but I wanted that "free" to be outside; I definitely did not want to let him loose inside the house. I had visions of this dove as a frantic missile pooping through every room, escaping each reach I made for him and any doors I might open. What could I use to nab him before opening the fireplace doors, or even how? In some way, I would have to encapsulate him.

I found some very large clear plastic bags and a large roll of masking tape. I taped a side of a plastic bag to the outer side of both doors and then very gingerly opened them just wide enough for the bird to fit through. I then sat down to wait and watch. I quickly jumped up when I realized I wanted to capture not only the bird, but also to immortalize it in a photo.

With camera in hand, a cup of coffee by my side, and snacks to munch on, I sat and waited. Finally, the bird felt comfortable enough to venture out of the fireplace and into the bag. I snapped a picture and quickly shut the doors behind him, trapping him inside the bag. I took the bag outside, put it on the ground, opened the seal of the masking tape, and waited for the pigeon to slowly make his way out of the plastic. I thought he would fly away, but he just sat there. Then I feared he was hurt and couldn't fly. I worried, *What now?* To my relief, he walked away from the bag and then flew up to the cherry tree for a brief stop before leaving.

I do have frustrations with my own animals, also. There are many stories of beloved pets whose antics and bothers, cares and scares, and aches and pains have tried my soul and my patience. Love the animals but hate the nuisance. Many of them frustrate me by doing damage to my property—shoes chewed beyond repair by puppies, sweaters destroyed by the repetitive clawing of a cat, upholstered furniture demolished by spraying or wetting. Troubles can be brought on by animals digging under, climbing or jumping over, or tearing down the pens that confine them.

Trapping an errant bird in my fireplace.
The top photo shows how I taped a large plastic bag to the doors
so I could safely capture the bird (bottom photo) and set him free outdoors.

Then there are the messes that occur just from the structure of the animal itself. Jude had an abundance of extra fur. My ex-stepfather-in-law, Gramps, fondly referred to as my outlaw, named this surplus hanging down her back legs as *flivers*. This baggage required periodic cleanup to clear out mats, tangles, and assorted hitchhikers. Yearly on the deck, I had a two-day job of combing out these bags of shedding fur. I had begun annual weaving projects with my art students, and I jokingly thought I should really learn to card and spin Jude's fur for weaving. My son observed, "Mom, why don't you think of getting a Lab next time, or some dog without so much shedding hair?" Did I listen? No. And several years later, the next dog would be another one of those "I should have known better—yeah, I should have listened."

My cats brought other troubles. Jzero not only walked in but also invited many friends to move in with her. I had never experienced any infiltration of pests before this time, and I was so slow on the uptake that the situation was fully developed before I realized what had happened (that ability of mine to ignore unpleasant things was operating again). I would itch. And get bites. And then I started noticing little black things in the bathroom. Jumping black things. Couldn't be fruit flies. Not in the bathroom. When I had remodeled it, I had changed the floor from a dark color to a very light beige, and it was there, as I sat on the toilet, that I first realized what was happening.

I was overrun with fleas so prolific I could sit and capture the little buggers between the flat sides of my thumbnails to squish them. I learned that unless I heard a crunch, they were not gone but lived to jump again. I squished, and I sprayed, and I squished, and I changed my bedding. And I changed it again and again. And I vacuumed floors and furniture. And I put pillows through the dryer. And then repeated the whole process several times.

I had replaced the window just off the kitchen with sliding glass doors that opened onto a deck. This made the next process much easier as I set up wash stations outside. After brushing and trimming Jude's flivers, I immersed her to the tip of her nose in water, hoping to drown the critters. Then I set dishwashing tubs on the benches of the picnic table. I still had the kittens and proceeded one by one to douse two cats and six kittens up to their noses. They looked like drowned rats, but I was gaining on the problem. It took several more washings with repeated sprayings over many days, but I finally conquered the invading hoard. And thankfully, I have never had that occurrence again. A few years after my flea infestation, I mentioned it to a friend who asked me, "What year was that?" When I replied it was 1981, she said she had had a similar situation that year and described her troubles and treatments.

She went on to add that her veterinarian said it was the worst year with fleas he had ever seen.

I recall that while washing the kittens, I kept singing, "I'm gonna wash that flea right out of my life and send it on its way." While singing and washing, I thought of our pattern of naming animals after music. This started with the first cat we had before moving to Virginia, named Nikolai, after the Russian composer Nikolai Rimsky-Korsakov. Laurie's cat Sasha was named after the duck in *Peter and the Wolf*, while Jude, of course, was from the Beatles's "Hey Jude." And so Kalija and Jzero just carried on the tradition.

The deck where flivers were cut and fleas were drowned.

28

MR. T SAVED MY DAY

*I*n the late 1970s, this was my first time living alone, and I was experiencing moments of mild unease at one end of the spectrum to sheer panic at the other. The Fife rapist incident had increased my anxiety and fear of intruders. One spring night, the neighborhood teenagers down at the other side of the pond held a graduation party and were outside playing games and having fun. They were loud, noisy, and running all around the neighborhood. I figured a lot of drinking was going on, and I started having ridiculous fantasies of wild invasions onto my property.

Yes, I had been reading way too many murder mysteries. Nothing had happened to incite such feelings except my own out-of-control imagination and insomnia. I found myself staying up later and later with projects. I changed the direction of my bed so I could see up the driveway, hoping I would notice if a car drove down at night. I dug out the foghorn inherited from my in-law's boat to keep by my side. I hoped raucous noise would scare away an intruder.

One night, a shrill "Help!" penetrated my sleep, causing me to jerk upright in bed. Although it sounded terrifying, this time I knew its origin. This call for help reminded me of my introduction several years earlier to a noisy feathered friend living in our neighborhood. This is how it happened at that time: My kids were staying overnight with friends, Bob was out on one of his three-month stints on the tugs, and with the house to myself, I settled down in bed for a long evening of reading. The window had been broken the day before from a backyard baseball game, but the glass had been cleaned up, and since it was springtime, I thought nothing of it as I snuggled back against the pillows. At around two o'clock in the morning, I was still riveted by my book:

Well, it was pretty bad. That wonderful girl—but you would never have known her. She'd been shot in the back of the head with a shotgun held maybe two inches away. She was lying on her side, facing the wall, and the wall was covered with blood. The bedcovers were drawn up to her shoulders.... she was wearing a bathrobe, pajamas, socks, and slippers.... Her hands were tied behind her, and her ankles were roped together with the kind of cord you see on Venetian blinds.

At that unfortunate moment, a shriek of extraordinarily high decibels assailed me through the broken window at the head of my bed. Rigid with fear, I rose up, every muscle taut, eyes bulging, and ears straining to listen to what might follow. I felt stress scrape my esophagus like sandpaper and acid creep up my throat. *What was that scream? Or who was that screaming? Was it inside the house? Was that down the hall? Oh, wait, I don't have a hall.*

At that point, I thought about the neighbor girl in the third house up the street, who last week had come home high on drugs and slit her heart open in the middle of her mother's kitchen. This girl a few years earlier had babysat my children. A shrill "Help!" again split the air, making my blood run cold. "Oh, shit!" I muttered, throwing the book across the room. Watching it slam into the wall and slide to the floor, I added, "This is no time to be reading Truman Capote. *In Cold Blood* can wait for the light of day." I apologized to Mr. Capote, sent up another prayer for the mother of the neighbor girl, got up, turned on every light in the house, switched on the TV, picked up my latest project, and started sewing.

The next day, my son told me the noise curdling my inner juices originated with a peacock. Off and on through the years, I heard these birds again, and a few years later, I discovered the source. Collecting for a muscular dystrophy drive along our road, I discovered a house set back behind the fourth house east of me. I walked down this private road, crossed a small bridge, and went through several acres of woods and clearings. It was a miniature wildlife retreat. In the front yard, I sidestepped ducks, geese, peacocks, dogs, and cats. That had to be where I heard the screech that terrified me.

A few years later, driving back from the nearby town of Milton, I saw a peacock run down Meridian and turn onto Twenty-Eighth Street. When I told a friend about this odd experience, he said peacocks have been used as guard animals. What a fun piece of trivia.

Back to the present. Hearing the shrieks for help tonight, I remembered the horrible sounds during the peacock's mating season. In disgust, I said, "Two o'clock in the morning and the blooming peacocks down the road are screaming their fool heads off!" I thought, *Even if I were a peacock, I wouldn't be turned on by that high-pitched cry.* I wondered if all those help cries I heard through the years were from the same party of peacocks. The internet lists their lifespan as twenty years; I don't know what it is in our neighborhood. I turned over, attempting to sleep.

In that hazy land of neither wakefulness nor sleep and still uneasy from the peacock cries, I recalled a story I had read to my students the year I taught kindergarten. It was entitled *Swimmy.* This precious story told of the sole survivor of a school of very small fish. Swimmy swam around by himself, very fearful as he darted away from menacing fish pursuing him for their dinner. He finally found a school of small fish like himself, asked if he could join them, and once more had a place to belong. This smart little fellow proceeded to convince other itty-bitty fish to swim in such a way as to form the shape of a very large one. They fooled the big predators into thinking that they were one great big fish—too big to be reckoned with. This was an idea that could be used by children who were being bullied.

When I woke up, I remembered a dream of working in the kitchen when three men dressed all in black roared in, shouting and ordering me around. They brandished ropes and weapons, threatened to kill me, and demanded to know where my valuables were kept. Tied up on the couch and trembling with fear of what was to come, I looked up and saw a strange contraption flashing eerie lights and floating down the driveway. The next thing I knew, Mr. T and Hannibal from the television series *The A-Team* hurled through the door, grabbed the men, threw them against the wall, pummeled them, and tied them up. Hannibal walked up to me, looked me in the face, and said, "There is no need to be afraid when you know you can take care of yourself."

After showing me some basic karate tricks, he walked out the door, threw the three men into the strange contraption sitting in the driveway, and drove away. I woke up thinking, "I don't have to be afraid of living alone."

I loved the over-the-top violence of that program because no actual harm was done and because it was all on the side of good. The good guys always won out and no real blood and gore were shown being spilled. I was sorry when it went off the air. The contraptions they constructed out of old parts for their weaponry also appealed to my sense of fun.

I was not afraid after my dream; I just imagined myself knocking into the next county and the next century anyone who intruded on me or my land. Yeah, I do love it when a plan comes together.

29

VOICE OF SPRING

In the middle of writing a check, my concentration was rudely interrupted. I looked up, trying to place the source of this disruption. Did I just hear a cock-a-doo-dal-do?

I laughed, thinking *I haven't heard that sound for a long time.* That lonely rooster crow in the morning set me to wondering about other animal experiences from beyond my own front and backyards. The third parcel of land to the east of mine reaches back the equivalent of four blocks, and through the years, it has been home to cows. A couple of times during those early years, we would see one of the Moriarity kids herding their escaped cows back home down the middle of the road. Of course, for many years, people rode their horses by our house. Regrettably, that is no more, but I still have the best of all possible worlds—a mile from freeways heading north, south, and east, and yet, the neighborhood still has a country feeling and, as I discovered when I started working outside on the land, I have my own private ecosystem. I don't need a summer or winter getaway, and I don't need to wander further than my own four walls and boundaries for adventure and fulfillment.

I live south of Seattle on two acres with a very compact woods, a small pasture, and my very own pond, but I did little with my land outside the house except for needed upkeep during those early years. I was busy with children, sporting activities with my ex-husband, and developing the curriculum for school. Then, on one particularly mild winter during these Middle Years, I moved my projects from inside to outside. I finally took the time to enjoy all the delights right outside my door, and I went to work reshaping the land.

As I put up fences, dug out gardens on all sides, and cleared the woods, I became more aware of the dozens of animals living there. Frogs and ducks, bunnies and crows, squirrels running and jumping across branches of trees, yearly visits by a woodpecker on a magnolia tree, hummingbirds on the honeysuckle bushes, a coyote across the backwoods, and two raccoons peering through the sliding glass door to see if this time I would give handouts. (Not!) For many years, a pheasant wandered across the west pasture, but he has long since disappeared.

One day, while drinking my coffee, I walked over by the sliding glass doors. Looking up, I saw something in the beam holding up the roof of my deck. I went out to look closer and saw that it was a baby squirrel. How did he get there? I had never seen squirrels this close around the house. He was sitting all by himself, and he looked at me with big, scared eyes. I could not figure out how he got up there and did not know if he could get himself down. Was he hurt? I moved a chair over and cautiously reached up to him, not knowing what he might do. He could not go sideways as the crossbeams were in the way. He let me swoop him into my hands and I cradled him while walking to the woods. I softly admonished him to go find his mommy and gently put him on the ground. He bounded away.

At a restaurant on the Puget Sound, I once looked out the window and was surprised to see ducks diving underneath the water. The water was so clear I could see about four feet to where they were feeding at the bottom. That is so different from the ducks in my pond at home. With little more than a foot of water, the ducks just tip over, tails sticking up in the air as they partake of their gourmet meal. From an article, I learned that our mallards are called "dabblers" because they prefer calm, shallow sanctuaries where they can sit on the surface, quickly stick their heads in while completely upended in the water, and grab a bite to eat. I read, "They dabble for invertebrates, fish, frogs, and a variety of plants." OMG—my ducks are eating my beloved frogs? Oh dear. Frogs? Ducks? How to choose?

I love to watch the whole process of duck life. The pond naturally fills with rainwater sometime in October and the ducks return. Every morning, I look out and count to see how many are there today. In the spring, there are about two dozen. Soon, the time comes when chasing begins and continues for several days. Then I see only drakes swimming and flying around, hanging out together, and keeping one another company, having deserted the females after the first week of incubation. The ducks have one brood per year: five to fourteen eggs in a down-lined nest in dense vegetation near the water. The incubation period lasts just under a month.

Soon after hatching, the young leave the nest but stay diligently with Mommy, following her in a little line into the water, diving promptly when in danger. They are able to fly sometime after fifty days. The young ducklings grow quickly and start having their own babies before they turn a year old. They have a short lifespan of around three years, so they reproduce quickly and in large numbers to maintain their population. Around here, they have a small survival rate with all the wild critters who are taking part in their own survival of the fittest.

I remember once seeing a fun video on the internet about a momma duck who laid her eggs on the awning of a store. When it was time for the babies to head to the lake, Mama scooted one of them out of the nest, off the awning, and onto the pavement several feet below. People who had been watching them from their office window went outside and caught the ducklings as they were ousted from the nest. When they were all safely on the ground, those people stopped traffic, allowing Mama to lead the babies safely back home.

One summer, my pond dried up quicker than usual, and I was worried about what would happen to the ducklings if they were not yet able to fly. I asked my neighbor across the pond what would happen. He told me about Mama leading them down past his place to the other end of the pond, across the road, and into Lake Killarney. I said, "If you see them, please give me a call. I would love to witness such a delightful happening."

The frogs arrive by March. Year after year, the highlight of spring, anxiously awaited and eagerly listened for, is the night when I first hear that noise—the raucous chorus announcing what I call with great glee "The Waking of the Frogs." I love it. I feel like a conductor. The night will be quiet, and, then merely by the simple act of sliding open the glass door, I start thousands of little tree frogs singing their hearts out— filling the whole neighborhood. What power. All from those delightful two- to three-inch-long green and brown creatures. The best frog chorusing happens on a warm evening after a rain, but individuals can also be heard calling throughout the day. Someone said that holding a singing frog is like holding the voice of spring in your hand. I throw parties to announce the waking of the frogs. I even bought a long green jumper, frog glasses, and a frog hat for those occasions.

Curious about this long-awaited symphony each year, I did a little research and loved one quote I found in *The Seattle Times*: "In a pond near you, thousands of small suitors are tuning up their voices for the annual swamp love-in." I learned some facts about my favorite natural inhabitants of the pond. In early to mid-February, male tree frogs begin migrating to nearby wetlands to establish territories and serenade females out of hiding. The males follow the cue of the lead singer for wooing—making those loud calls generally described as a "rib-it" or "krek-ek." Males make these sounds by inflating a single throat sac that swells to three times their head size.

Females might listen for days before coming to the ponds to choose a mate. As soon as a female draws near her favorite crooner, the male jumps on her back and wraps her in a hug called *amplexus* (Latin for "embrace"). They may stay conjoined for several hours as she swims through the reeds. After "the hug," the female attaches a quarter-size gelatinous mass of ten to seventy eggs to stems or sticks in shallow water. As the eggs are released, the male fertilizes them. The female leaves the pond within the week, while her mate may stay up to a month, seeking to extend his genetic reach.

Long frog toes topped with round pads make them expert climbers, even on vertical, smooth surfaces. One day I gasped in horror when I saw a little tree frog that had been on the screen when it was closed was now a dried frog fossil. I saw a brown frog one day and remembered hearing that the frog population was dwindling. Afraid that something was wrong with the ecology of my pond, I hurried to tell the science teacher at school. He said, "Relax. That is normal. In most species, the color varies with the temperature and other conditions, with hues ranging from olive green through bright green to brown. This frog can change color from one hour to the next, often blending in with the natural background." He also told me that Pacific tree frogs live in every county in the state and were recently named the official Washington State amphibian.

Well, they are behind the times; they've been my amphibian choice for years.

30

A FOWL WEEK

*I*t has been a fowl week. First off, I woke to a sound announcing our yearly woodpecker visit. Old "red-top pecker boy" was back, hammering on the pine stump not far from my bedroom window. While he reached out with his long sticky tongue, hoping for breakfast, I wondered what grubs he was getting today and if sap served as syrup for the other ants and beetles he might be finding.

Nearly thirty years ago was when I first heard a continuous loud *tap tap tap* out back. I went outside and found a woodpecker setting up this terrible racket, banging his bill against the back corner of my house. My first thought was the possible ruination of my home. After listening to the peculiar sound for a few minutes, I remembered the siding was asbestos; of course, he was not going to go through that material. Shortly afterward, red-top came to the same realization and moved around to the front yard where he set to work on the trees.

Through the years, he, his children, and grandchildren have used their strong yellow bills to drill and drum uniform holes up the length of all four trunks of the magnolia tree. All around the trunk and several branches are spirals of holes just the width of his beak. That poor, misshapen tree is allowed to grow at will, suffering not only from a lack of formal pruning but also succumbing to periodic wild hacking of those branches growing in the way of the house or people. Oh, but its blossoms—every spring they are beautiful to behold. And the leaves, left on the ground to decompose, leave gorgeous skeletons. They are works of art by themselves and are included in my collages for display inside my house after their demise outside.

Intrigued by these noisy creatures, I read that woodpeckers have developed a number of adaptations to prevent brain damage from their hammering. A small brain size maximizes the area between their brains and skulls and limits the duration of the hammering contact. A built-in membrane acting as goggles closes right before their contact with wood to protect their eyes from flying debris. And a nose mask of special feathers covers their nostrils. I discovered another strange configuration peculiar to their eating habits: Their first and fourth toes face frontward while the second and third ones face backward so they can grasp and walk vertically up a tree trunk. Their short legs and stiffened tails aid them in getting their food and building their nests.

After reading these facts, I realized not only how very adapted they are, but also that as many times as I have seen woodpeckers chomping on my trees, I have never seen them flying to or from their feast. Oh well, figuring out why is for another day.

The loud and very distinctive caw of crows has become frequent in the last few years. As far as I'm concerned, these are the least likable of the noisy feathers in the neighborhood. These new kids on the block arrived in my area a little over a decade ago, bringing with them hordes of previously unknown and disgusting weeds. The ones I hate the most have sprung up all over with no concept of zero population growth. There is a plant with long, skinny green branches creeping and crawling over everything. It multiplies as it goes and can end up several feet long. Its different names give a clue to one of its worst characteristics—cleavers, stickweed, catchweed, and grip grass. Its little green leaves stick to anything they touch, and they give me an itchy rash, but the worst part is its multitudes of seed pods. These little brown balls covered with miniature hooks hang onto everything, like Velcro. No wonder they spread so badly.

The first time I weeded a wooded area filled with them, I was wearing a sweatsuit. When I went into the house, I realized I had acquired an armor of seed pods clinging to almost every inch of me, including my hair and the insides of my socks and shoes. They would not shake off. It took me an hour to pick those little critters off by hand. When I described these offenders to someone, she said that they might be what are called cleavers. Yes, they were.

I have been known to feed my animals on the back deck, but not for many years now. I don't want to attract opossums, raccoons, or crows. The neighbors feed their five dogs on their back porch, which faces the window above my computer. When I stop my writing to search for a better word, I look up and see the crows swooping down and eating the dog food placed out there for their delight.

A few years ago, when reports of West Nile virus were circulating, I ran across a dead crow. Putting it into a plastic bag, I called the announced phone number to report it. I never heard back from them and finally threw the corpse away.

I have heard the saying, "Know your enemy," so I read about crows also. They often score very highly on intelligence tests. Northwest crows have modest linguistic capabilities and can relay information over great distances. They live in complex societies of hundreds of individuals who have various "occupations." One species will drop seeds onto a heavily trafficked street and wait for a car to crush them open. Tiny video cameras mounted on crow tails have shown them using a variety of tools. They will pluck, smooth, and bend twigs to get at a variety of foodstuffs. A teacher at my school would regularly report on the happenings of a large number of crows who frequented the area outside her classroom. She told of their intense rivalry and mid-air jousting, like playing chicken to establish pecking orders.

On the opposite end of my bird like-dislike continuum are feathery hummingbirds. I remember one incident years ago when my children were babies, and I was at my parents' house. A hummingbird was trapped in a corner of their porch. He was having no success at escape because two sides were enclosed by glass. I walked up to this tiny fluttering, frightened creature and easily captured it in my hands. I was so surprised—initially by the fact that I was able to catch it and then at the activity I was experiencing from its tiny body. I thought it was fear causing the frenetic pulsating against my hands.

With a little reading, I discovered they flap their wings fifteen to eighty times per second and, to support this rapid beating, they have the highest metabolism of all animals to sustain this frantic activity. Their heart rate can reach as high as 1,260 beats per minute. Well, no wonder that little guy was trembling in my hands. I also learned they can hover in mid-air and are the only birds able to fly backward.

I love to see the hummingbirds feeding on the honeysuckle plants alongside my front porch and over the railing at the back of my deck. They also help control the insect and spider populations. Their bills open slightly for their long tongues to dart into the honeysuckle flowers. They visit hundreds of flowers daily to consume the requirement of more than their weight in nectar each day, and even with this, they are always only hours away from starving. Makes me tired just reading about their frenetic lives.

A marine biologist friend visiting one day looked out the window and said, "There is a crane in your pond." Sure enough, one of those most majestic of creatures was honoring us. He stood in the middle of the pond holding his proud head on that long neck with such practiced grace. His movements looked like a choreographed dance. His presence seemed to speak volumes, and I thought of those people who give out the message of being entitled, as if saying, "I really do deserve a crown." Those large, long-legged, and long-necked birds fly with necks outstretched, not folded back onto themselves like the similar-looking but unrelated herons. My friend added that their lifespan may be several decades. This was another feathered friend surprise after many years of living here. I have now seen four of them.

Blue herons have made a few periodic visits from their habitat a few miles away at the bottom of Peasley Canyon. I did a little research and found this area had been reported as having the second worst polluted stream in King County before 155 acres were drained to build a super-mall with parking for nearly nine thousand cars. Mill Creek, formed by Lake Dolloff and Lake Geneva above the Auburn Valley, was already the victim of sedimentation from housing construction and natural landslides from above, while downstream, a buildup of reed canary grass and other vegetation slowed water movement, reduced oxygen levels, and raised water temperatures above state standards in the summer. Well, the blue herons seem to have their own economic difficulties and are traveling less, also.

One day I was initially thrilled looking out the window to see Canadian geese in the pond, but upon reflection, I sucked in my breath—*oh no.* We are two houses west of their migratory flight path where they twice yearly honk their way north or south. Within a mile south, there is a flock at Fivemile Lake, and about four miles north, the Weyerhaeuser Company headquarters sport more. But I had never had any come to call on me before. On this day, four of them called a halt to their migrations to make a courtesy stop in my pond. They are so beautiful, and I enjoyed the novelty of watching them, but I did not want them to stay. I have seen the slime and mess they leave behind, and I do not want them to turn my pasture and lawn into a skating rink. Thank goodness, they did not return with their friends and relatives to take out squatter's rights.

When I drive by Weyerhaeuser and notice the dozens of Canadian geese, I start wondering what makes the difference as to where they go. And why they go? How are the decisions made when there are hundreds of them? Do they follow a leader? Is there an alpha goose? Do they collaborate? And is it decision-making or pure instinct? What happens when they don't agree—do they have a goose negotiator? Or a mediator? And is that a younger-sister goose doing all that loud squawking?

And then came my afterthought—*oh, please don't make that decision, however it is made, to settle in my pond.*

31

I Can Coexist—
Yes, I Can, Except...

*W*orms are great little critters and especially to be admired for their talent of growing new halves, although I just read that may be a myth. How terrific it would be if we all had such powers. I like to watch the bright green inchworms work their way along a branch, and I think it is very clever of them to color-coordinate with their surroundings. I have seen brown, red, white, and green worms, but in Virginia, I was surprised to see a bright blue one on the porch one day.

The insects in the garden I ignore, letting them do the jobs their nature decrees. There are usually cutworms around, Japanese beetles on the zinnias and sunflowers, and aphids on the nasturtiums and tomatoes, in addition to all the other inhabitants. We all get along just fine. Bees, of course, are to be welcomed anytime, anyplace, just for who they are as well as for their pollinating and honey-making functions. They are abundant outside the windows of my kitchen and where my computer is set up on the east side of the house, and they seem to particularly like the cotoneaster thriving there. Visually, they provide such wonderful graphic opportunities for cartoons.

There are other animal constants that trigger in me neither love nor hate but are simply cases of coexistence. These are the ones who do not harm me, and I do not harm them—usually.

Spiders follow along those lines. As well as eating insects, they serve an aesthetic purpose, creating beautiful webs on the posts of my deck, which, with dew or rain, turn into abstract works of art, looking like sparkly rhinestone jewelry. I wish I could find a way of capturing these fleeting art galleries; recently I have photographed a few.

I once read a newspaper article about the combined effort of thousands of spiders collaborating to build a massive web covering bushes and trees in a canopy reaching two hundred yards. Scientists determined that twelve different spider families built this larger web, so they had more flies and bugs come dinnertime. You gotta admire that collaborative endeavor, the ability of those vast numbers to coordinate their efforts to accomplish a task. I wish we could take a page from their instruction book to work together so well. Yes, good coexisting creatures do exist. Listen up, government.

Ah, but—the yellow jackets and the ants. I coexisted with these little stinging, biting machines for several years until my hands-off-the-chemicals policy allowed a population explosion tantamount to our deplorable world population. Oh, there would always be one, two, three, or four yellow jackets that appeared when I was having a summer dinner party on the deck, but I could live with that. And one year when I was painting the exterior of the house on a tall ladder, one zeroed in on my rear. Since my startle factor did not kick in and I did not fall off the ladder, I was still able to coexist and leave them be.

Then came a year when hired workers indicated that they would not work at my house unless I cleared out the yellow-jacket nests. After the second story was put on the house, I no longer chose to clean the gutters myself since I did not want to risk falling both stories. My gutter man stopped in the middle of the job one day, came to the door, and told me he would be back to finish the job when my eaves were rid of all those nests teeming with yellow jackets. The following year, the man who works wonders cutting my trees down, chipping branches, grinding stumps, and digging ditches down to the pond also told me to get rid of the yellow jackets living under the shed roof and in a pile of logs.

As for the ants, I began to notice steady streams of them running up and down the trees in the backwoods and inside an old tree stump. I also saw them making endless forays along the one hundred fifty feet of ivy beside my driveway. And then I noticed a big anthill in the backwoods, one up by the road, and two in the little woodsy area to the side of my driveway. In fact, one cone-shaped hill measured two feet across and stood about that high. And all were filled to the top with frantic, fiery little red ants. I knew they would chew me up in nothing flat if given the chance, and they did periodically bite me while I gardened along the drive.

I recently read a *National Geographic* article on research being done on swarm theory. It asked, "How do the simple actions of individuals add up to the complex behavior of a group? How do hundreds of honeybees make a critical decision about their hive if many of them disagree? What enables a school of herring to coordinate its movements so precisely it can change direction in a flash, like a single, silvery organism?"

It was just like those thoughts I had about the hundreds of Canadian geese. There one day and gone the next, as I wonder who decides and gets to be the boss. And if there is disagreement, who gets to override the others? A male is, no doubt, also the decider of goosely activities.

I also read that a single ant or bee is not smart, but the colony has a collective intelligence. With this swarm intelligence, the colony solves problems unthinkable for individual ants: Find the shortest path to the best food source, assign work, defend territory, organize highways, build elaborate nests, stage epic raids, and defend their territory.

No one's in charge of the ant activity. No generals are giving commands, and no managers are directing. Now, that's my kind of society—to have it all work out just right but with no one bossing, saying it's wrong, or insisting on their way. Maybe I'll put in to be an ant in another life.

Swarm intelligence involves simple creatures following simple rules and acting on local information. Nobody sees the big picture. Now that I wouldn't like; I prefer to see that big picture. Those using this method bump into one another and communicate by touch and smell to determine where the other has been so they will know who their encounters have been with, such as foragers, maintenance workers, or patrollers.

In fact, learning about ants, bees, and spiders has helped us better manage our world. Collective intelligence has influenced airline-boarding procedures, spy networks, robotics, and crowd behavior. A company in Houston, Texas, uses an ant-based strategy to manage complex business problems. Oh, would that Congress take a page out of the ant manual.

Back in my own little world, it was time to override my earlier decisions to coexist with pests out of regard for the planet's ecology. I do believe in survival, but I began to get rid of the ant nests and lower the hornet populations.

The yellow jackets move around each year. While working the land, I run into their current homes, which may be attached to the eaves of the house, carport, or shed, and they may nest in piles of wood or even in the ground. I have found them nestled among the *Ajuga* and heather. One year, I even discovered a nest under several sheets of plywood left through the winter after the donkey shed was torn down.

I once shoveled the remains of a pile of wood chips on the back of my property. These were the results of a particularly wild winter with many branches broken from my trees. The chipper man had worked his wonders, giving me a huge pile to periodically distribute onto my paths and gardens. I was down to the composted ground level of this pile when I ran across a section filled with ants. I did not particularly want them building their apartments in and around my squash, so I changed course and brought out pans of boiling water to deter their building plans. I thought of a fact from that article I read: There are one million ants for every person on Earth. It felt like my entire share was here.

After drowning all the visible ants at one end of the chip pile, I continued to the other end, hoping to find it non-antsy. No sooner had I lowered the shovel when I was immediately bombarded by dozens of very angry yellow jackets swarming from a small hole in the chips; they were not at all happy with the threat of eviction from the home they had so diligently built and tended. Having had great success with the boiling water on the ants, I thought, *Hey, why not give it a try with the yellow jackets.*

Oh yes, still not looking ahead with adequate information of consequences. I did not give thought to one vast difference between ants and yellow jackets. Both can bite or sting like crazy. Both are hard workers in building their little fortresses and both do not like their work to be attacked. Both are angry and feisty little critters when disturbed. But, I learned the difference between the two; it is in the range of mobility. After bringing water to a boil in my big canning pot, I trudged out to the back pasture and poured it down the hole. A hoard of angry beasts

An exceptionally intricate, beautiful wasp nest
I preserved as a natural sculpture.

tore after me. I had ignored that very important fact—the yellow jacket can fly. Ah, consequences indeed! When will I ever learn?

After applying baking soda to the carnage of stings, I regrouped. I have not often been accused of giving up on my ideas easily; yes, I admit to stubbornness. I thought if I had something to cover the hole so that the yellow jackets could not get through but the boiling water would, I might have success. Success, that is, without putting myself as well as nature in harm's way. Getting one of my silkscreen frames from the studio, I placed it over the hole and tried again. I had no better luck than the first time, as the determined critters crawled out from underneath the screen.

Now sporting a new batch of baking-soda spots, I gave up and admitted defeat. Off to the store I went to buy the dreaded aerosol poisons. That was the year I learned the wisdom of using the spray at dawn or dusk when they are all cozy, tucked into their nest for the night, and reading their bedtime stories, no doubt. Since discovering that valuable information about timing, I have been able to go back to using boiling water and not the environmentally harmful poisons, and I have not been stung since.

However, I have kept the treasures of the many yellow jacket nests I have gathered, one nearly a foot high. I have one from a laurel bush along my driveway, with a small branch and leaves built right into it. I like its fragile outer-parchment-like coverings with undulating waves of soft grays, browns, and tans. But this outer coat needs to be removed to reveal the intricate internal high-rise structure with story after story of hexagonal shapes, each built on stilts and each containing hundreds of miniature compartments for the larva.

In fact, the first nest I opened still had wiggly, squirmy white grubs in their little individual bassinets on the top floor. After some thought, the art teacher in me came through, and I poured Elmer's glue on them to preserve my new sculpture. I heard the faint whimper from one little fellow: "Oh, dear, I was hoping we were on the endangered species list."

32

No Redeeming Love:
Flies, Slugs, Moles

So many animals in my life. As a general rule, I love God's many creatures; however, my own internal animal barometer slides on a continuum from the extreme right, marking deep-abiding love, to a far left, bordering on hatred. It travels all the way from welling-up, heart-bursting, eye-flowing, loving remembrances of those special pets who stole my affection through the years to an outright smash-mash, pouncing on with a gleeful "gotcha." This is always accompanied by a somewhat guilty "Sorry, God" because of my wonder and gratitude for the blessings of their world of nature. This sliding scale of mine has a multitude of spots between the two extremes, each spot bringing its own variety of emotions.

My hate-hate animal stories are on the no-redeeming-love side of the scale. These are the ones where I apologize to God while, at the same time, I exterminate his creatures. Fat flies are disgusting in the kitchen near my food or circling around my sweaty head as I work outside in the summer. Mosquitoes are pesky and a nuisance, buzzing around my arms and face if I stay outside working into the dusk.

But never were we "bugged" as much as in Virginia. Bugs, bugs, bugs—creeping, crawling, flying, jumping, buzzing, croaking, fluttering—little, big, and enormous bugs. Even with screens over the windows at night, the walls and ceiling could be covered with insects of different sizes, shapes, and colors, with varying numbers of feet, wings, and antennae length. They were thick, they were all over, and they were most disagreeable. When my small children came in from playing in the sand or the woods, they might have chigger bites, another new and unpleasant experience. And bath time activity, besides playing push-off-to-shore, included picking ticks off each other.

The garbage can could not be near the house, we could not eat outside, and if the kids ate Popsicles on the carport, the drip spots soon became thick with flies. Flies flew in every time the screen door was opened, and, of course, try to keep young kids from going out and coming in—to go to the bathroom, to take a quick TV break, to play a game, to hang on the refrigerator door and survey the perceived inadequate contents within, to get a drink of water, to hide from the boys, to hide from the girls, to say hi, to say good-bye.

A couple of years later, I would teach a kindergarten class in the Pacific Northwest during an autumn that was thick with big, fat, slow flies. Lunchtime would be particularly bad, and I hate flies inside at all, much less around food. Each day that fall, I would take a rolled-up piece of newspaper and fasten it at one end with a rubber band. I would then have great fun entertaining the children as I hammed it up, dancing around the room and swatting at flies while yelling, "Take that, you dirty fly! How dare you come in and disturb these children—they deserve to eat in a clean place!" The children would roar with laughter while I had fun acting like a fool until the flies were all gone, the room was once more pleasant, and we could get back to work after lunch.

Lower on the scale than mosquitoes but on a par with flies are slugs, moles, and mice. I am not usually one to question the ways of nature; however, I cannot fathom these creations. I do not want to coexist with slugs, and once I learned that when hacked in two, they do not multiply like I believed worms did, I began attacking them without mercy and with any sharp tool at hand. Every year, my poor dahlias have to poke up out of the ground about three times before they get up the energy to try again in their battle with the slugs, or until I finally decide to be consistent with a daily attack on those disgusting, creeping slimers. I now walk around in the early evening with a glass of wine in one hand and a shovel in the other for whacking them into pieces.

Slugs sometimes crawl up on the deck and into the herbs growing in a wheelbarrow there. I have seen slimy trails up the side of the house and, on occasion, have found a dried slug just inside when a door was left open. When my son was under two years old, I was working in the yard and turned around to see him lifting a slug on the way to his mouth. With a shriek and a loud "Yuk!" I lunged at him, grabbed his hand, and stopped him in time. It took a long time to get the slime off those tiny, delicate little fingers without hurting him, especially with those fingers attached to a wiggly, squirming little boy who saw no reason for the fuss. Fifty years later, the thought of a slug going into his mouth still makes me gag.

I mentioned the slug story to him one day and he told an even worse tale. One of the girls he went with early in life told him of eating a slug when she was young. He said he could no longer kiss her.

Moles are an ongoing and constant hate story on my land. I will often be walking somewhere and feel the ground caving in under me. The pastures and yard are becoming like dirty bubble wrap but without the fun of bubbles to pop. I worry that the concrete slab under my studio will be undermined; I fantasize it slowly slipping into a mole cavern. Several times a year, a different mole range will erupt somewhere. It looks as if metal bowls of dirt, tied together on a rope, have been buried, and then some unseen force flies over them with a gigantic magnet, oozing them up from the ground.

When I am mowing the pasture, I need to zigzag so the wheels will mash down the mounds of dirt without ruining the mower blades. And, when the mole path has been through the gardens, I need to stomp all around my rhododendrons, azaleas, and heather to keep their roots from an agonizing death by air exposure. Even the gravel driveway is not immune to these underground invaders. I found this out when lying flat on my back after the leg of the ladder I had been standing on to prune tree branches sank into a mole hole.

A friend of mine said I should rent a cat. Her cat, Bentley, has caught several moles and her neighbors tried to talk her into renting him out for their yards. She said that Bentley would lie waiting, watching for hours with his arm down a mole hole until one came along. My cats catch birds and mice; I wish Bentley had talked to them about conquering moles.

Several years ago, after seeing an ad in the paper, I called and hired a "mole man" to catch those pesky tunnel-boring machines. We talked about price but did not discuss what would happen when the mole was caught. Sometime later, I came home from school and was heading toward the front porch when I realized something very strange was hanging from my doorknob. That funny, creepy feeling started up, the one I get when I suspect something is not going to be pleasant, but I will have to deal with it anyway. I walked closer, peering at it, still not comprehending what the rather soft, misshapen, hangy-down thing was. It was not a solid hard-edge form, so I knew it was not the new telephone directory. Coming closer, I distinguished a clear plastic bag containing furry dark brown with parts of pinkish tan. When I recognized a foot, my brain started clicking in with the request I had made of the mole man; I realized a dead mole was hanging from my doorknob. For some reason, I never called him back for another capture.

A woman in my writing class once wrote a story about catching and keeping a mole in an aquarium. They planned to make a video of it eating a worm while, out of the range of sight, her granddaughter would crunch on carrots for sound effects. The day before the designated filming, the mole died. They discovered the silicon on the aquarium's corners to be the poisonous culprit.

I thought, *Well gee, that's how I could have used my old fish tank— only instead of moles, I could have started a slug farm.* I used to put out pans of beer in the vegetable garden, but that makes a terrible mess. I have also used salt. I let my mind get silly thinking of putting salt out for slugs, even on the road, and jump ahead to imagining the car slipping on slippery, slimy slugs, causing an accident.

And then, of course, my response to the policeman's disbelieving query: "Ma'am, what did you say caused your accident?" *Oh, officer, it was entirely the slug's fault.*

33

THREE STOOGES:
STRAIGHT, KINKED, AND KNOTTED

I have received many of my animals from my daughter, and in June of 1996, I agreed to take three female kittens that her momma cat had delivered. When they arrived, I admired the coloring of these three adorable little babies. One was a calico with a better placement of colors than my former three calicoes, the second was black and white, and the third was all black except for the smallest showing of white hairs on her chest. I looked at these recent arrivals, oohed and aahed, as I do with all baby creatures of any species, and then I did a double take—or rather, in this case, a triple take.

The calico's tail was straight and moving around like a normal tail, as would be expected. But, when I looked at the black and white kitten, I saw that its tail sported three permanent kinks. It looked like someone had taken a pair of pliers and bent it in those three places. But the black kitty's tail was even more extreme. It was all curled up, with only the tip sticking out at the end. It looked as if someone had tied it into a knot.

Laurie said that was the way they were born, and later, on their first visit to the vet, he concurred, "Yes, that was the case."

Like most women, the Three Stooges had never particularly en-thralled me, and I remembered little of my junior high school visit to one of their movies except their names. But upon seeing these kittens and their tails for the first time, I thought of—and immediately decided upon—the names for my new crazy-tailed darlings—Curly, Kinky, and Moe.

The kittens were fun, as all kittens are, and they enjoyed playing together, until one day I came home and Kinky was missing. This was in the middle of a five-year remodeling fiasco of adding a second story to my house. And, after finally getting designs, permits, a new septic system, and a second contractor recommended by a friend, I erroneously thought my life would soon be squared away so I could retire. This second contractor, a very strange little man who I found to be dishonest and thoroughly untrustworthy, had talked me into paying ahead and then walked out on the job. He had been interested in my animals, and I always wondered if he took Kinky. Many times, I have thought of driving by his apartment to see if I could see a cat there—my kinky cat.

When I am sitting at my desk working on bills, planning, organizing, or studying, Moe will walk from one side of the desk to the other on top of the papers right in front of me, swishing her tail back and forth in my face. When I am writing or working at the computer, as I

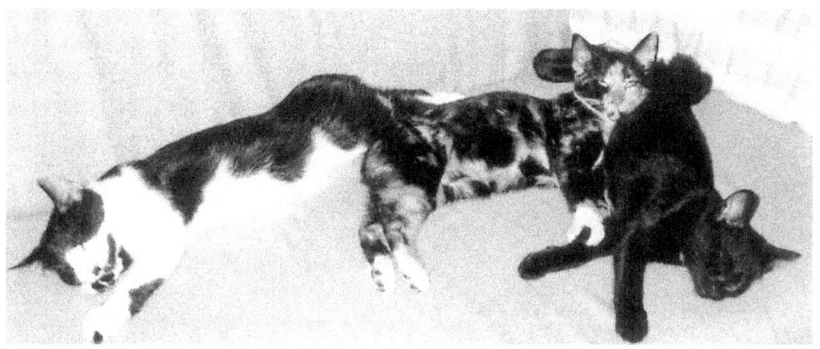

My trio of kink-tailed kittens: Kinky, Moe, and Curly.

am right now, there is Moe lying in my work-to-do basket. We both love baskets. I love them for their looks, as decoration, and also for storage, while Moe loves to climb into them—whether they're little or big, full or empty, or on the floor, a stool, a table, or a shelf—to lie on top of the magazines, papers, clothes, or books within them, either to watch what is going on or go to sleep. It is so funny to see her sound asleep with her back to the activity, her face right up against nothing, and her paws curled under her.

From this view of her top and back, she looks to be all of one color, a mottled rust and brownish black. When she is standing or sitting up, you can see the pattern of a beautiful white bib and chest, white paws, and rusty tan down her legs. I found the name for this calico to be doubly appropriate when a friend stated that she thought Moe's name was short for Mosaic.

The most serious of the cats, she appears to be contemplating the worries of the world. She will sit and look straight at me without blinking or looking away for the longest time. I find myself asking her, "What? What is it? A penny for your thoughts!"

Then again, she was the one who later watched me as I disposed of an opossum; maybe she is remembering something, and it's best I don't know what she is thinking. They say cats work out your karma. That is what I think when she is lying on top of my chest, looking me straight in the face as I lie on the couch reading.

I started a bunny-breath check for cats coming into the house after one interesting day. Curly came up to the sliding door with something hanging from her mouth. I thought, *Oh no, what do I have to deal with now?* I gave a small shriek and went out to see what needed rescuing. Curly very obligingly dropped her present and looked up at me with that expression of, "See, Mommy, what I brought you."

It was a trembling baby rabbit. Curly had treated it very tenderly, and I picked it up and explained to Curly that while she was a good cat, the bunny would like to go back to his mommy and siblings. Seeing them near the edge of the vegetable garden, I took the bunny there. Later, I saw them running around as if playing tag. They must have thought they were safe here. However, when Moe started down to join them, I called her back. I told her that Curly was our security guard, and since she was out prowling the perimeter of the place, Moe didn't need the same job description.

Curly gave new meaning to an expression I had heard many times during my high school years of participating in physical education, the Girl's Athletic Association, and the tumbling team. When I would indicate in some way my super-sensitivity, I would hear the teacher yell across the gym, "Don't get your tail in a knot, Corfield!" I now had a cat with a real tail in a knot. And some knotty tales to tell because of it!

Curly was still a young kitten when I heard a terrible yowling from the end of the deck. Stepping out the door, I saw her clinging with her front paws to the arbor post, paddling helplessly with her rear legs, her curled-up tail caught in the vines of the wisteria plant. Since it was impossible for her to straighten out her tail, this left her flailing in the air, unable to escape. I was able to cut the vine and free her, but the experience was painful for both of us; I landed some pretty good scratches, and she, of course, was terrified, as well as having a very tender tail. I did not want to think about what would have happened if I hadn't been there.

The next time she got hung up was even more traumatic. I had left one of my paintings leaning up against the dryer, and when Curly jumped down from the windowsill above the dryer, she knocked it over, breaking the glass and catching her tail in the hanging wire on the back of it. This time, my gardening gloves were nearby, and I thought to grab them before taking a firm hold of her to extricate her from the mess she was in.

I had to twist and turn her tail to get it out from the wire. I was unwilling to go for wire cutters, as this would leave her loose to flail around in the broken glass. She was howling in heart-wrenching wails, trying frantically to escape this horror she was in. I had her head in a death grip, working to release her tail. Just as I got her free, I was, for the first time, able to take in the whole picture. I nearly fainted when I realized that her face had been within an inch of a large shard of broken glass. Realizing I could have rammed her face and eyes into it, I, weak-kneed, was finally able to let her loose.

Curly was also my predator cat who gifted me by bringing dead birds and mice to the mat on the deck. Then she started taking it a step further. I turned the heat off when I went to bed, loving the fresh brisk air of an open window. I spent the half hour between getting up and leaving for work in the bathroom, nice and cozy, with a little space heater. Because I turned the house heat on before leaving for work, I arrived home to a pleasantly heated house for the evening.

That is, until my little killer cat disgusted me once too often. My bedroom window comes down to bed level with my bed turned sideways up against it. This way, I can see the lights of a car if one comes down the driveway during the night, and I can see the moon travel across the sky from my bed. Curly slept on my bed until she felt like hunting, and then she scooted the blinds apart to climb out the window.

Curly with his bent tail.

On her lucky nights, she would climb back in the window, carrying a mouse—who was sometimes still squealing—across my bed to the floor near my head, where she proceeded to eat the whole thing, except for the spleen. That I would find in the morning to clean up.

One night, I had had enough. After getting so stressed hearing the shriek of mouse and crunch of bones, I got *my tail* in a knot, also. I went out to the living room and slept on the couch. That was the last time I allowed the cats free rein to go in and out at will during the night. Thinking ahead and not wanting the noisy consequences, I put the screen back on my window and determined we would all stay in for the night.

34

No Redeeming Love:
Mice and Opossums

*M*ice have caused me many uneasy times throughout the course of my life. I am not afraid of them, but I do not tolerate them well either, and I hate them inside my house. The first sighting or perception of any mouse-like evidence sends me into a frenzy of tracking down every dropping, catching all the critters, covering any possible entry, and washing every dish, pan, or linen of possible contact. The whole time, my grousing—complete with expletives—can be heard around the block—if we had blocks. I have learned that mice will chew through linoleum but not through adhesive tape; they will not brave steel wool, either. Information that is welcomed by everyone, I am sure.

My earliest memory of an interaction with a mouse was rather funny, but I don't think the rest were. In junior high, I was told to sweep our front porch. There were about twenty steps up to it, and it was about six feet by six feet with a turn to the right to go through the door into the house. Going out with a broom in hand, I startled a mouse unwisely taking a rest outside the door. He looked at me, eyes bulging, and started running. When he ran out of the porch, he continued to pump his little feet as fast as he could as he hurled through the air before landing twenty feet away in the brush down the hill on the other side of the driveway.

My next memory was not so fun. I was twenty-two years old and, along with my two babies, was living with my folks while I finished my college education. During the addition of a second bathroom, the upstairs was not closed in, and in the middle of the night, I heard a rustle, lifted my head, and saw a mouse run across my pillow under my face. I remember being so stressed out and angry that even thinking about it now increases my adrenalin. I got up and slept the rest of the night on the couch in the living room.

From 1994 to 1999 during a five-year remodeling fiasco of my own house, an area was left open while the upstairs was being added. Many birds and mice took this as an invitation to come in out of the cold and attempted to make themselves welcome. I believe they also set up an advanced communication system to inform their friends, relatives, and enemies about this generous place where they could avoid the elements during the ice storms of 1996 to 1997. However, Puget Sound Energy and I conspired to fool them—I had no power or heat for seven days.

Remodeling does try my patience and during this time, I captured many bodies, some in rather strange places. At two different times, during the obligatory cleaning and vacuuming under and behind the refrigerator, I found a mouse dead in the coils. When I stopped to think about it, I was very relieved that it was dried rather than rotten, moist, and full of maggots. Nevertheless, I could not rest until the area had been vacuumed, wiped down with vinegar, and blessed by the pope—in absentia, of course.

Two must be a magic number—or a cursed one—because twice I discovered mice in my washing machine. My laundry facilities are very centrally located, and I have a habit of leaving the washer lid open so I can toss towels and clothes in as I go by and not run a load until later. When I was ready, I didn't consider looking through the clothes to check for mice any more than I would think to check for giraffes. Later, when moving the clothes from the washer to the dryer, I ran across a dead body. Needless to say, I ran that load of clothes through two more wash cycles, minus mouse, before relegating them to the dryer for real.

Another time, I found a live mouse racing around and around the inside of the washer, this time without any clothes in it. During my brainstorming process of how to dispose of him, I briefly considered running him through a wash cycle as a way to hurry his demise, but I opted for a more conventional method and picked him up by the tail to throw him outside. I was very glad to finish the remodeling, have the house closed up, passed by the inspector, and consequently, as a by-product, warmed up. I have not seen a mouse or evidence of one since. Well, except for the ones brought in to be shown off for Mommy's approval by one of the cats.

Nor do I want to coexist with opossums. My experience with them has not been pleasant and I would dump them all on the next train headed back south. When I lived in Virginia, I decided that the movement of animals must be akin to the Southern drawl, because there were continually animals, from turtles and cats to dogs, raccoons, and opossums, lying dead along the road. They seemed to just move more slowly than in the Pacific Northwest, maybe because they don't need to get in out of the rain.

I have lived in my house in the northwest corner of the country since the spring of 1966, but it was the 1980s before I became aware of opossums in this part of the world. I was introduced to them as roadkill on Military Road near my house; a few years afterward, I had my first encounter with a live one on my land. Putting the second story on my house necessitated bulldozing for a new drain field on a section of my backwoods. Before that clearing, there had been a den in a pile of branches and brush; each time I raked it down and filled it in, the hollow would appear again. When I first saw the opossum, I figured that was the animal I had ousted from there.

I was taken out of my comfort zone one day when I reacted impulsively in a way that surprised and shocked me, because I thought it foreign to my nature. One day, while stacking wood at the edge of my carport, I picked up a log and stopped cold. Staring up at me with unblinking eyes was one of the ugliest of God's creatures, right on a par with deep-sea fish and magnified cockroaches.

Now, I am very territorial. On a couple of occasions, I have been known to be what might be interpreted as mean-spirited, and I do not take kindly to intruders on "my" land. That pink and tan critter with the big pink snout and long naked tail, looking like a cross between a pig and a giant rat, stayed absolutely immobile, looking at me without a blink, and was very deserving of the term *playing possum*. I swung my arm to shoo him away. He did not respond, not a twitch. I yelled and stamped my feet. No response. I hate lack of initiative. *Do something! Speak up for yourself! Don't just lie there!*

Standing there in our stare-down, I started to think about Jzero, my aged and beloved cat, never one to roam, who had disappeared during the year. "Did you get her?" I asked the naked lump in front of me. And then I remembered her two babies who had disappeared earlier. "Did you get them?" I asked accusatorily. Continuing the same line of thought: "I have three new baby kittens." That spurred me into action, and without further thought, I picked up a nearby two-by-four, hit the thing with several hard whacks on the head, dug a hole at the back of the property, and buried it far away from the sacred site of my beloved pets.

I gave no more thought to opossums until several months later, when gardening in my front yard, I turned around and saw one, sitting there, still as a statue, watching me. *Not again,* I thought, and, walking up to him, I hit him over the head with the blunt side of the shovel. Turning around, I saw Moe, the most mature of my three cats sitting there, looking at me with her usual Moe look. The one that says, *Yes, I am the one working out your karma.* I could just see her gears turning. *Oh, Moe, what are you thinking? Are you glad I got rid of it, or did you think you could play with it?* I looked closer at her and could almost hear her say, *Yikes, I'm thinking I better watch my step around here.*

When I think about that beady-eyed little monster who might have destroyed my Jzero, I am filled with loathing. I do not like that opossum; I do not like its little skinny, naked-looking tail. I do not like its indolence, its nonactivity, and its nonexpression. Doing nothing and expressing nothing are the ultimate in play-dumb—passive aggression par excellence. Maybe because it's so opposite to what I am so often about—reactionary, impulsive, loud. No, I have no redeeming love. Yes, I am opposed to opossum.

35

MORAL DILEMMA:
WHO IS THE SCOREKEEPER?

O ne night, I got up from the couch to throw another log on the fire and pull the drapes closed against the storm rumbling outside. Lying back down, I reopened *Accidental Mother* by Rowan Coleman and read,

> *Carrie made choices decisively and rode them out no matter what happened. Sophie never chose what happened in her life—she let fate choose for her and never questioned how different things could be.*

Sticking my finger on the page, I fell back against the pillows and stared at the flames igniting in the fireplace. I muttered to myself, "I need to think about that a bit," and let myself tune into how I make my decisions. I thought, *It's almost as if I have led my life on automatic pilot. As if some other person were pushing the buttons on my control panel.* And then I remembered the ring I had bought yesterday. Looking down at my finger, I thought, *Boy, that is prophetic.* Called a decision ring, it has an inner part that turns upside down, showing either a diamond or a sapphire depending on the direction the inner movable part is facing when I put it on.

I started asking myself questions. *What is moral? Who decides such things? And how are they decided? For any situation, would there have been a different solution? If different, how so?* And then, *Why?* I continued asking questions about decisions I have made: *Would I make a better choice now? What is the moral, right thing to do? And, right for whom?* I keep broadening my thinking to include moral dilemmas of more far-reaching implications: *When do you put an animal to sleep?* I consider how different animals are brought to their demise and ask, *Who has that right?*

Then I began thinking about negative comments I heard this morning when I told a group of people about my killing two opossums. *Was it ethical to kill them?* I carried my inquiry further: *Was I wrong to not want them on my land? Well, what about the mice and the moles? And the flies and mosquitoes? The ants and yellow jackets? Does the size of the animal make a difference in the morality of killing it? Is there a cuteness scale? Does gracefulness or beauty count? Flies, mosquitoes, beetles, and cockroaches are no problem for most people. Mice in the house—well, why not? But opossums in the woodshed and, all of a sudden, it becomes cruel? The evaluator of my actions thought so, anyway.*

I looked back on other decisions I made regarding the animals in my life. Where do you *draw the line?* Where *do* you draw the line? Where do *you* draw the line? A person could make themselves ill or immobilized by going around in endless circles about making choices of how best to coexist in our world.

I kill a rodent or insect and say, "Sorry, God." Is that hypocritical? Just where on the fence of life's questions do I sit? I try to live a moral life; I try to have regard for the world I live in and for the creatures of that world. At times I choose to have more regard for myself than for those critters that make my life difficult. So many experiences with animals involve conflicting feelings. They require making choices that, from this point in life, I might make differently than I did in my earlier years. Then again, I might choose to make the same decision but with a new awareness.

Is there a way to balance things out? Once an action has been taken, does any other action "even it up" or counteract it? What about the fact that I have spent a lifetime carrying spiders outside to release them? Does that even the score? *Is* there a score? And *who* is the scorekeeper?

Like who's in charge here, anyway? Who gets to decide? Is there a ladder of importance for who makes these decisions? Is your decision more valid or worthy to follow than mine? We can all declare *this* book or *that* expert to be the one to follow. Ultimately, we are still the ones accountable because even if we follow someone else as *the* way, that is the decision *we* make. Or I could just flip my decision ring and go where it takes me.

A squirrel in our rafters.

Which animals and what reasons matter? Is there a hierarchy of valuable animals, a rating scale of worthiness in the animal kingdom? Does God delineate between the creatures in His or Her world? There are those who think that humans are superior. Some beliefs hold this life as irrelevant because a version of afterlife is all-important. I wonder: Are the ones making these decisions affecting the ecology of our world? What determines the tilt of the scale this way or that way, and for which animals? Who *is* more important?

There is a question of rationale. I didn't want opossums on my land, pure and simple, but is that a good enough reason to kill them? Was my fear of their killing my three little kittens enough? There are those who say that killing of any kind involves bad energy and is wrong and immoral.

What more could I have done? For the first time, I considered that I might have called some agency to come to get the opossums. I really doubt I would have had any success, but I could have tried. Options, efficiency, problem solving—those are qualities I so admire. Why did I not think of trying more avenues than reaching out and knocking the objectionable creatures over the head? However, I would argue that I did not put any objectionable chemicals into the world to kill them.

Does attitude make a difference? I wrote about swatting flies with glee. Does that make me a bad person? Why would that offend? Is a fly any deader or less dead with no attitude attached to his demise? Everyone makes their own way to decide the rights and the wrongs in their world. Maybe I need to rethink my philosophy of where I fit into the universe. In the fourth grade, realizing that I fit into a very large whole, I wrote my name, my PO box number, the name of my county and my state, the "United States of America," and then, yes, the "Universe." I knew even at that time that I was a little speck of dust in the dirt pile of life. And I have tried since to keep the dirt that is in my keeping in good shape for those who will come after me.

I would think a major importance in making choices would be the aftereffects—the consequences. What were the effects and to whom? What are the consequences of a two-by-four to the head of an opossum as opposed to pesticides and herbicides sprayed across the land, changing the makeup of our food supply, affecting the lungs of all who come in contact with them, and contaminating the land, water, and food supply for future generations? Everything has a degree of consequence.

I think what I have been missing is the acceptance of myself for the choices I make. Maybe I should turn my decision ring—to self-acceptance.

36

THROUGH THE TELESCOPE OF TIME

I stopped, paintbrush in midair, to look up at the TV. A newscaster was telling of a remarkable family who had a little Chihuahua born without front legs. This loving, caring family had kept him, rigging him up on a cart with wheels so he was mobile. I watched that little critter pushing his contrivance around from one member of the family to another, getting hugs and kisses everywhere he went. I was bombarded by contradictory feelings. Thoughts came pouring in as I reflected back in time to Virginia when the children and I chose our first cat.

I put down my paintbrush, set aside the drawing board, and let myself go back forty-four years to that long-ago incident. We discovered the condition of a kitten that we had on impulse brought home for Laurie's birthday. *Should we have kept that little deformed kitten? We would have been able to keep it. I did not think so at the time. And ... we didn't.* I broke out of my reverie and wondered again about drawing lines—other than ones on the drawing board. The lines where decisions are made. And how those lines can be drawn in so many different ways.

In the way of coincidental incidents, it was only two days later that I saw a video on the Web of a two-legged greyhound. Running around in a field, he actually caught a Frisbee even though both of his legs were on one side. When he was very young, he had lost the other ones during a car accident and learned to maneuver just fine without them. I wondered if he would have been able to shift his weight and balance so well if he had been older when the accident happened. I think probably not. But again, maybe so. Who knows?

A short while later, I received an email about two horses. One had a metal leg and the other was blind. The one with the metal leg led the blind one as they moved around the pasture with their heads touching each other. I began to get a feeling—you know, the one that niggles in to whisper, "Could this be a conspiracy against me?" The one where

I am supposed to feel guilty. Or … maybe learn an important lesson?

You say potato and I say pot*ah*to. Back in my reverie, I thought of the different ways people do things and of the attitudes and opinions that influence those choices. Each person's priorities can be so different from others—fifty people might have fifty differing opinions. And the attitudes of any one person change through the stages of a lifetime. My thoughts and choices have definitely changed over the last fifty years with my experiences. Back in the beginning, I would never have even considered these things.

One person's idea of expediency could be another person's declaration of cruelty. One believes that nature will take its course, while another makes use of every pharmaceutical invention known at the current time. An animal might be put to sleep when it first becomes an inconvenience, or it might be kept to die in its own time, even if that time is drawn out and painful. Anyone who has had a pet has made decisions regarding euthanasia. When a dog or a cat lives eighteen years and its health is rapidly declining, what is the choice to be? And *when* is that choice to be?

Then again, what is the choice with a nine-year-old dog whose health is rapidly declining because of parasites not responding to any treatment given? Would it be the same? And how would the choice of the moment be tempered by the dog? Thinking of Jude and how I had wished I had made the choice earlier rather than waiting for the day when she could not get up … earlier than when she peered up at me with such a sad, imploring look. I didn't think I had done her right. Because of that indecision, Jude spent time in pain. That choice affects me now. I would not know until a decade later, when I made the choice differently to put a beloved pet out of her misery earlier, that I would still feel agony and guilt. I decided that might just be the nature of me and not the happening with the animal.

I don't give myself credit for what I might be capable of because I've never put myself to the test. How do I know I wouldn't have loved that little underdeveloped cat with as much care and regard as my other cats? You do what you can at that time. I have worried so about the choices I made and have equated my decision with fearing that I am a less caring person than those people with the two dogs I heard about. Is that the case?

We all have different approaches. How blunt and honest should we be or how much should we hide our true feelings in the effort to be "nice"? How much will we bend to the politically correct phrases that bombard us daily? One person's style of care for another can be perceived as an infringement on the dignity of the one being cared for. I think those who pamper and speak to animals as if they are imbeciles are disregarding the very nature of the animal to serve their own needs. And where in the middle would be the lineup of cats and dogs dressed up for Halloween that I saw in the email? Should the priority be respecting the nature of the animal or the novelty and attention received by the owner? The breeding of ugly dogs and their extremes of size, temperament, and other characteristics for the attention they give their owners would fall in here somewhere, also.

I thought back to that oft-expressed term from my father, accompanied by his stern inflection, "Explain yourself, young lady." But I don't have to explain myself, or try to, anymore. There is no Right Way that I must decipher. I can quit dangling out here trying to figure out what anybody else's Right Way is. The way I thought I *should* do "it"—"right enough" or "well enough" is where I would finally feel at peace. All I have to do is decide what I will do and then stick by it as being valid for me. My choice about the cat in 1964 was made with thought and care for the cat as well as us. It was an okay choice. My decision ring is my individual right to choose for myself.

37

A Log of Barking

For the most part, my experience with animals has been with the pets of my household or with those wildlife critters I either enjoy or are inflicted on me by the natural world around me. This chapter involves frustrations built up over time without even knowing the individuals. I am not proud of myself when I do not like animals beyond my boundaries, but I find it hard to avoid when I receive repercussions from them.

These stories mainly involve neighbors and their cats and dogs. My count of their dogs has reached somewhere in the neighborhood of fifteen, with a wide range of yips, yaps, arfs, woofs, yowls, and howls often emanating from their direction to the east of me. I do not know what the bark count is at the present time.

I think back to the first time I saw neighbors to the east. I was digging a new section for my driveway. They stopped their car and asked me if it was safe to get out with the odd-looking dog in their future driveway. There have been some strange individuals living in that house, but those immediately before these current neighbors were great people. The woman cut hair in her home, and it was very convenient to walk next door for that chore. There was a very sweet grade-school girl. And all right, Steve could be seen sitting out in his shop smoking pot once in a while in the evenings, but he did keep the blackberries and morning glories from getting out of control and inundating my land.

The dog in question was large and exotic—possibly an Afghan hound. It was slender and tall with long, very slinky, silky fur hanging down around its face. It was sweet, not to be feared, and never caused any nuisance or disturbance. I hardly knew it was around. I have remembered that early hesitation and fear several times in the years since while the current parade of dogs come and go—and yap through the night. At that time, I did not know that ten years later, a Doberman owned by these new people would claw my legs, leaving puncture wounds and scars.

I admit that, during the same time, a total of eight cats and two dogs lived in my home. After some fifteen years of faithful service, Jude died three months before the neighbors moved in, and shortly after their arrival, my two calico cats died of old age—Kalija was eighteen and Jzero close to that. I was without animals for a couple of years, and then a little-bitty, light-gray bundle of personality purred her way onto my land and into my heart. She was scraggly, scrawny, and flea-ridden, and, when taken to the vet, was found to have worms. Once all the required business was taken care of, I named this wee one Smudge. She was light gray all over except for a darker shape on her face. At the time, I wondered where she had come from, but the neighbors had been gone for about two weeks by then, so I figured she had been let out by someone from the road. Jzero had also wandered in that way and stayed close by for all those years.

The mysterious Smudge, the disappeared cat I missed.

I became very attached to this little bundle who always curled up on my chest as I lay reading. Some weeks later, I was cleaning up the carport with Smudge close by my heels when the grade-school boy next door said, "That's my cat." I told him that when she had been left here to fend for herself, I took her in and paid a vet bill to the tune of ninety dollars. I asked, "Do you want to ante up for that?" He replied, "I'll ask my mother." He came back shortly and said that I could keep the cat. Not too long after that, Smudge disappeared. I never saw her again. Oh, how I wish I knew what had happened. One of those situations of "I don't really know"; I will never know.

Actually, I guess the first of the animal incidents occurred with the cat they had when they moved in. He decided to take his daily naps in my car when I left the windows open. Another one of those "You didn't learn your lesson, did you, Dianne? Why didn't you start closing the window?" Then he made a habit of coming in through my bedroom window. I had enough when he crawled into a space between my waterbed and the wall and wouldn't come out. I poked in from one end of the space with a broom, thinking that the cat would go out the other. He didn't. I couldn't move the waterbed without emptying it. Finally, I called the man next door and told him about the situation. I implored him to come and retrieve his cat. He finally did manage to get him out of there.

In the early days, before I put up fences around my land, every day for two weeks their spaniels would come down and knock over my garbage can. I was tired of picking up garbage from the space of the twenty feet they scattered it. So, I went down to G.I. Joe's and bought a combination BB and air gun. I tried it out in the back by shooting at a tree in the woods, and, finding that I was able to operate it, I put it beside the back door.

My unplanned timing turned out to be perfect. The next morning, I saw the dogs come down onto my land; I grabbed the gun, went out to the corner of the house, and pumped it in preparation. It just happened that the neighbor was outside getting ready to leave for work. He heard the action of the gun, looked up, and saw me sighting down its barrel, looking ready, he thought, to shoot one of his dogs. He quickly called them back, and I had no more trouble with the garbage cans. Just to clarify, I would not have shot the dog; I just wanted to scare them away. It was even better to scare the neighbor into keeping his dogs away himself. I believe that was when they installed the gate at the top of their driveway.

There were fun things! These neighbors are a sports-oriented family, and so often through the early years, fun noises of play of three children infiltrated my property. Also, the noises of planned sports activities with groups of friends and relatives in their large, well-kept front yard would come floating across the boundary. I would think, *Oh, can I come and play, too?* I have smiled many times as I've thrown different kinds of balls back up over the bank.

It was so neat on one hot summer day when my twin great-grand-daughters were visiting and were invited up to swim with the neighbor's granddaughter. We so appreciated that and later invited the girl along on our Tacoma Musical Playhouse and dinner excursion.

Then began unsolicited nightly entertainment. A nightly canine orchestra—a quartet of boombox caliber. The canines in residence at that time included two large black dogs of an unknown breed who had replaced the spaniels. The third dog was a white newcomer larger than a Saint Bernard, with brown marks around one eye and his other ear. He was the bass of the quartet, emitting the loudest, longest, and lowest woof imaginable. The fourth was a little-bitty, yappy brown creature which must be the "in" dog of current fashion. I surmised this since a metal sculpture resembling it stood by their door.

Barking had always occurred next door and at any time I gardened on that side of the house, took the garbage out, went to the carport, or when company came. By February it had become excessive in volume and duration, continuing through the night. I had trouble sleeping and was losing all tolerance. I needed my sleep.

I called the county to determine my options. I found out a barking nuisance is defined as "any domestic animal that howls, yelps, whines, barks, or makes other oral noises in such a manner as to disturb any person or neighborhood to an unreasonable degree." And that "any person who allows an animal to be maintained in violation of this chapter is guilty of a misdemeanor punishable by a fine of not more than two-hundred-fifty dollars … and/or imprisonment of a term not to exceed ninety days … or a civil penalty up to one thousand dollars." I started a complaint against them and began to tally the times of the dis-

One of our neighbor's dogs loose on our land.
This fellow was larger than a Saint Bernard.

turbances as I had been instructed. I kept a notebook by my bed as a log of barking. I called other neighbors to find out if they were also bothered, and I composed the following letter, which I sent to the offenders:

> *Night after night, your pack of dogs keeps me awake. There can't be a purpose for keeping them outside to bark at every squirrel, coyote, or other creature that happens to prowl around. They set up the tirade if I dump my garbage, go up to get the mail, and move from room to room, and it seems to occur even when I turn over in bed. It is enough to have them barking during the day and crapping on my land as they go through. I don't need their chorus all night long.*

> *It is so pleasant when your dogs are gone or are put inside with no barking after eleven o'clock, such as was the case last night, the sixth of February. But the night before, Thursday, was a more usual happening. They barked almost continuously throughout the night, making sleep impossible. If you are going to have all those dogs, please put them in at night. Sleep deprivation is serious, especially*

for older people, those with medical problems, and those who are sick. Being awakened several times a night (supposing one is able to get back to sleep each time), night after night, with no letup, is serious. Others in the area have also been awakened. Please give some consideration to the welfare of your neighbors.

And I signed it.

When the neighbors were contacted by the county, the barking during the night for the most part stopped for a time. Recently, two new terrier-type dogs and a Doberman have been added to the mix, and the barking has started all over again. After a couple of phone messages, there is a curtailment of this unsolicited concert, but only for a short while. What can I do? How can *I* train my neighbors to train their dogs? Maybe I need to talk to the dogs to train their owners.

Years later, I was to find these same neighbors would have a better attitude than I had shown. My daughter would start bringing her huge and loud German shepherd when she visited. Tied up on a run line out in my woods, she would often loudly express her displeasure at such horrendous neglect and restriction. I learned that the neighbor would go over and talk with her. Oh dear, another lesson for me to learn.

38

IF ONE IS GOOD,
ARE TWO BETTER?

*W*hy do I have such love-hate relationships with so many things? Especially my animals! This thought came to me one day when I couldn't ignore a large crash interrupting my soak in a hot-tub escape with a book. I realized I could not stay oblivious to the consequences of some animal's current mischief, so I got up out of the hot tub and dribbled across hardwood floors to see what was happening now. The wind was blowing up a storm, and as I opened the sliding glass doors, my skitzy fifty-pound husky came hurtling through to escape those wind monsters.

The hot bath had followed several messy cleaning jobs. I had finished emptying the shop vac of dog hairs. Before that, I had extricated one of my least favorite critters from under the fridge during the necessary periodic cleaning. It was still a time of remodeling, so I had found a dried-out mouse. Thank goodness it was not rotten with maggots, as were the squirrels, moles, opossums, and mice I found outdoors from Sitka's hunting sessions. Since I was at it, I dumped two dead bird parts off the mat outside the door on the deck. No, that one I can't blame on Sitka. That was from one of the cats, probably my little curly-tailed predator.

I had had nearly twenty years with Jude and her yearly shedding of bulky flivers, those vast amounts of excess fur around her hind legs. And of course, my son had cautioned me to get a Labrador retriever next time. But no, I didn't think about that when, six years after burying Jude, my daughter's part-husky and part-wolf mix named Chanka had pups, and I said "Yes." Laurie had been the source of Jude, that beautiful and mellow companion over a long period of time, so I knew that animals from Laurie were good to have. In June of 1997, one year following the arrival of the three kittens, I took in two of Laurie's female pups, who looked identical except for a slight difference in the width of white down the middle of their noses.

Juneau (left) and Sitka (right).

After the fact, I called a good friend in Alaska who was very knowl-edgeable about all animals, and I asked her about huskies. She said that her partner, Vic, had lived with people who raised huskies for the Idi-tarod race, and that he was now out sledding at a dog lot, one that had Lab pups for fun but also eighty-five sled dogs. Well, Tina informed me about huskies, and, as my granddaughter would say, "More infor-mation than I wanted to know." Tina's assessment included, "They are independent and do what they want, love to wander, tend to roam, will dig anywhere, escape confinement, and they not only shed but also do it all year long."

It was another one in my long life of "I should have known better" moments. And another of many "I should have asked—and listened—before the decision" times.

I was torn in my choices for names but settled on Sitka and Juneau. I had heard that dogs should have short names with no more than two syllables, and I was happy with my choice. However, when I later learned about dog behavior patterns, I came to think of Sitka as Houdini, as she could escape any confinement, and Juneau as Genghis Khan, since she loved to roam.

My animals had never been restrained on my two acres, and I hated to start now, but in the last fifteen years, several housing developments were built near our area, and traffic increased. By then, it had been more than ten years since the paper girl delivered newspapers on horseback and quite a while since any horses had gone by on the road. That time was gone forever. I was still working, and I did not want these very active young dogs to run free and leave the land, so I built a twenty by twenty-two-foot enclosure with a six-foot-high cyclone fence.

However, the best-laid plans were set aside: Juneau was a digger and would work industriously to get under the fence, and Sitka would simply go over it. I never saw that happen and wondered how she climbed up it. One corner of the fence had a roof and sides for protection, but I didn't see any way for her to get up to the top of that. Sometime later, the neighbor said that he had seen her go bounding over in one leap on the driveway side. There was an added obstacle of a

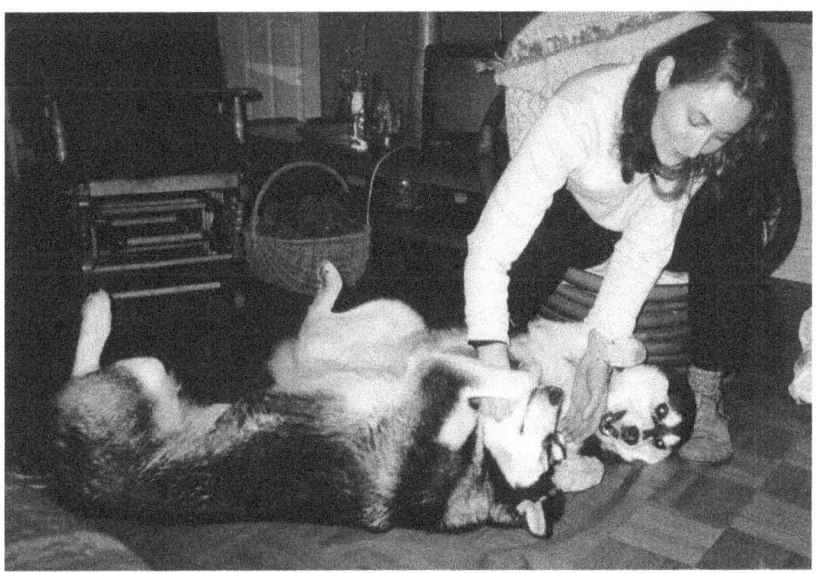

Laurie playing with Sitka and Juneau.

kerria hedge on that side that she cleared, too. I bought some additional fencing, rigged it up at the top of the original fence to angle it in so that Sitka could not get over the top, and placed some concrete blocks where Juneau had been digging.

In February, when they were a year old, I was driving down the driveway after school, and I noticed the dogs were not in their pen. Going in my front door, I looked straight through to the sliding glass doors leading onto the back deck, and there I saw Juneau sitting in a very peculiar fashion. When I opened the door for her, she hopped in on her hind legs holding up her front paws limply in front of her, looking like a rabbit, with a pleading look on her face. I did not need to be a rocket scientist to know I needed to immediately pick up my fifty-pound bunny very carefully while trying not to hurt her more than she obviously was already, put her in the back of the wagon, and go directly to the vet. As I lifted her up, carried her around the house to the car, and headed up the driveway, I kept looking right and left for another black-and-white bundle, but Sitka was nowhere in sight.

As I thought, both of Juneau's front legs were broken, and I set in motion the needed surgery for repair with a pin, splint, and cast. Leaving Juneau "unpained" on drugs and in good hands with my very reliable veterinarian, I set off for home to hunt down Sitka. I could not find her anywhere around the house, on the land, or up and down the road. No Sitka. At dark, I finally gave up the search and went inside to get myself some dinner.

A short time later I thought I heard a whimper and remembered that because of the remodeling, a crawl space under the kitchen window was left open. I grabbed a flashlight to see if that was where she had gone. Sure enough, when I aimed the light into that small opening on the side of the house, I saw her about six feet back. She was trembling and wore that same pitiful imploring look of animals in distress. I knew she was injured and in pain, but I could not get her to come out. When I tried to scoot under the house to at least pet her, she only retreated further. Not wanting her to go any further away, I stopped coaxing and left food and water just outside the opening. By this time, it was quite late and very dark, and I did not know what to do. If she would not come out for me, then she would definitely not

Juneau and Sitka injured.

come out for anyone else. I went to bed weary and heartsick for a night of very little sleep.

I was overjoyed the next morning to find Sitka out from under the house and in the yard where I could reach her. It was obvious she was not okay. She must have dragged herself on her front legs from under the house as her rear legs were not working and she could not walk. I picked her up as best I could and took her to the car. The vet said her pelvis and her hind leg were broken and she should have a specialist to the tune of at least two thousand dollars. With a large expense already committed for Juneau, I could not afford to add that amount. The vet said that he could amputate the leg. I was ashamed of myself, but that was unacceptable to me. He then stressed he wanted me to hear very clearly what he was about to say, and he went on to emphasize that he *wasn't* saying this, but that he could set the leg himself and let nature take its course. I said I am a great believer in the powers of nature, and that is what I chose to do.

I would love to give my vet a medal for his matter-of-fact attitude and easygoing nature in the middle of such a traumatic situation for me and, of course, such a painful one for my dogs. He always showed concern but with confidence and competence in the handling of animals. He also put me as much at ease as was possible to do with a worrywart like me.

Juneau and Sitka during their long recovery.

No one ever stopped in to say they had hit the dogs; I never heard anything about what had happened to them. I had to assume that they escaped through a hole that Juneau had dug under the fence and that they both had been up in the road together and were hit by a car. They had to have gotten themselves the two hundred feet from the road back down to the house, and then around to the back in the broken condition they were in. I don't know how Juneau could have hopped like a rabbit on her back feet or how Sitka could have dragged herself all that way. The only other explanation would be that some extremely mean-spirited, horrible person came onto my land and lambasted them with something like a baseball bat. I hate to even think about that case scenario.

When I brought them home from their respective surgeries, I set up a hospital ward in the living room. I put my cushions from the papasan and deck chairs on the floor on top of the floormats. Their food and water dishes were moved in, and except for periodic visits outside, they were quite willing for some time to lie around and recuperate. The next month, we all went back for X-rays and a checkup, and with time they healed well. However, the ordeal had taken its toll on me as well as them, and I realized I could not think of keeping both of them. They were so identical that the thought of separating them was difficult; I have always had a special affinity for twins, and in fact, in later years, I would be a great-grandmother to two sets of identical twins. But Juneau and Sitka's having some wolf in them worked against me. Together, their loyalty would be to each other and to their own shenanigans instead of to me, and as they got older and wiser, it would be even more difficult to keep on top of things.

My son mentioned my plight to his vast array of friends, and he told me that one of them was very interested. It was ideal since his friend had fenced-in acreage and other animals for company. He came to see the dogs and was very taken with them. I told him the situation, explained the full extent of their injuries, and then gave him a choice. He chose Juneau. At a later date, he stopped down with a much heavier Juneau and asked if I could part with Sitka also. I said, "No."

We have many moles, and Sitka will lie in wait with her full attention to some spot in the ground, then suddenly spring up, pounce, and, in true husky fashion, proceed to frantically tear at the dirt, heaving it in all directions. I know she has caught a few since I have found her carrying around or chewing on disgusting carcass parts. When food has been sitting too long in the refrigerator to be safe to eat, I think, "Oh, I'll give it to Sitka." Then I stop and wonder, "Well, if I'm afraid to eat it, it could hurt her, too." Then I remember the grisly dead bodies she has dug up, cuddled up to, bitten into, carried around the yard, and hidden in her hidey-holes for safekeeping for yet another day of munching. Then I stop worrying about the delicateness of her digestive system. Of course, my stomach nearly empties when I see her choice of menu.

In the fall of 2000, during my yearly pruning of trees at the top of the driveway, I was standing on a six-foot stepladder, trimming the lower branches of a cottonwood tree. I was usually very careful to position the legs of any ladder I climbed on to ensure that they were level and on very hard ground. The multitudes of moles leave many soft places in the soil. Since this was a gravel driveway, I assumed it would be hard. *I know, never assume!* And another *when will I ever learn?* I was at the top of the ladder when one leg caved in and I fell straight back, landing flat on my back on the gravel. I was conscious the whole time,

Grandchildren Shoshannah and Josha with the huskies.

but for quite a while, I could not move. I guess this was what they call having your breath knocked out.

I was 190 feet from the house, where there was no person present anyway, even if I were able to call out. I was about twelve feet from the road with cars going by, but fir trees stood on both sides of the driveway, and to see me, passersby would have to be going very slowly, looking at right angles at exactly the moment they were passing my driveway, and be heading west so as to be on my side of the road. I felt very helpless. Since then, I've called a friend any time I plan to prune trees or go up on the roof for some reason.

While I was lying there waiting to be able to move again—or hoping I would be able to—I thought of the stories of Lassie from my childhood and of how she would bring help. And there was my skitzy Sitka jumping and bouncing around, barking, nearly frantic, and knowing that this was all wrong and yet not having a clue of what to do to help.

Oh dear, skitzy and clueless, also. But I definitely loved her anyway. I could *soooo* relate.

39

Looking Ahead,
Walking into the Next Century

*M*y Middle Years era was coming to a close while the end of the century approached.

Happenings that occurred during the 1980s: Mount St. Helens erupted, the Cold War was coming to an end, an 8.1-magnitude earthquake shook Mexico, Japan Airlines had their worst-ever single plane crash, the space shuttle *Challenger* disintegrated, the Chernobyl nuclear disaster happened, the *Exxon Valdez* ran aground, and we experienced huge social and economic changes while I remodeled, landscaped, and continued to teach. And I watched *The A-Team, The Cosby Show, Roseanne, Seinfeld, The Golden Girls,* and *Cheers* on television and saw *E.T.* in the movie theater.

Through the 1990s came political correctness, the beginning of cable television, mandatory seatbelts, Walkmans, boomboxes, and the explosion of PCs (personal computers). The Information Age with its new media was changing our world forever as the Internet, digital cameras, flat-panel TVs, and mobile phones came bursting into our lives. *Pretty Woman, Home Alone, Northern Exposure, L.A. Law,* and *Murder, She Wrote* entertained us, as did Rollerblades, light-up sneakers, ripped jeans, combat boots, and grunge music.

As those years rolled by, my granddaughter and grandson were born, and my son and daughter each built their own homes from the ground up. It was so fun to see my children become adults in their own right—earn a living, make a home, and create interests, activities, and hobbies. I remember the first time I realized while visiting my son at work that he was an adult who had come into his own, not only responsible but also respected by his employers and employees. Wow, my serious, big-eyed little fellow was all "growed up" and what a good job he had done of that chore. I so admired him. Later, I would spend a day in my daughter's second-grade classroom and have the same experience with her soft-spoken, caring interaction with her second graders. This generous, talented lady had set up a home-away-from-home in her classroom and given so thoughtfully and conscientiously to her students.

I thought back to a time riding with my children while they learned to drive. I reached a point with both of them when I finally decided they knew what they were doing, and it was safe for me to sit back to enjoy the scenery—I could quit sitting on the edge of the seat, swiveling my head in every direction to look for obstacles we might plow into or vehicles ready to assault us. How wonderful to have good, caring, capable, and responsible children, and I was blessed with many opportunities to see them and to care for grandchildren.

I also learned I could live alone just fine, and to prove it to myself, I spent several holidays by myself without being part of a family group. During these Middle Years, Daddy and Gramps died, Gran had a stroke, and Mother reached ninety years of age. In August of 1995, fifteen years after wandering in, Jzero disappeared. She had always stayed close to home and never wandered off as Kali did. Always petite and frail in her older age, I thought an opossum, coyote, or raccoon got her. That same year, after eighteen years, I had to have Kali put to sleep, and she joined Duchess, Jude, Kookla, and Sasha in the pet cemetery in the back pasture. Another era of animals had come to an end as well.

There was solitude in living alone; I enjoyed having no demands, orders, or directions. I chose what to do, when, and how to accomplish it. I dreamt of hop, skip, and jumping across the sky, pretending I was running from one cloud to the next, or sitting on a moonbeam watching the world go by. I enjoyed dinners and trips with friends, and I often held Friday happy hours after work in the hot tub on my deck with what I called the Sac Six—three of us sitting on one side and three on the other with a board across the middle holding our hors d'oeuvres and wine.

My teaching time was also in the closing stages as retirement drew nearer. The question was *what would I do?* I needed to figure out the later years of my life. I considered holding art workshops and retreats and not only built a studio, but also added a second story to my house for two more bedrooms and a second bathroom. While I remodeled, I listened to Jennifer James, Laura Schlessinger, and John Bradshaw's *Homecoming: Reclaiming and Championing Your Inner Child* for life lessons missed.

During this period, I was given much to think about with pets inside and animals outside; I started asking questions and thinking hard thoughts. Once those thoughts started, they kept coming as I made association after association. I was realizing how each choice had narrowed the options left.

Why had I lacked the skill all my life to think ahead with the knowledge that tomorrow will follow with consequences? Is there a DNA connection for not looking down the road? I had lived my youth without a thought of later cost—to me, to my children, or to animals. I marvel now at people who early on have made choices based on solid, thoughtful goals and plans, those who worked all their lives toward what they wanted. That seemed so far out of my frame of reference. Shaking my head, I thought, *I can't even fathom that*. I hadn't seemed to choose what happened in my life according to any overall goals or plan—it just seemed to choose me without my awareness—until I was midway through it. Or often, not until completely through it.

I had a fleeting fantasy of all those revelations flying at me through the air, arriving like insects to pile up on the car window—I would end my road trip through life with the sum total of my awareness splatted in spot after spot like a Jackson Pollock painting on the windshield of my existence.

At last, I cleared out the supplies I had accumulated from thirty-seven years of teaching (twenty-five of them in one room), retired from my job, and finished the second-story remodeling project. On New Year's Eve with the turn of the century looming, I watched TV millennium celebrations around the globe and rejoiced that the world and I had survived. I remembered as a child thinking I wouldn't live that long, but here I was, looking forward to my Later Years yet to come.

My beloved home in Auburn.
Purchased in 1966. Remodeled by 2000.

PART III

SHIFTING OUTLOOKS

FUR KIDS PROLOGUE

I turned off the kitchen light and headed into the back room where Richard, index finger perpendicular to his lips, quietly shushed me. I jutted my chin forward, eyes opened wide, and head slightly to the side, indicating, also without noise, "What's up?" He pointed to the sliding glass door. Looking up, I saw the sensor light had turned on to lighten the darkness outside. There sat a feral cat who periodically prowled around outside. We had seen her before, and I wondered why she should bring about such a reaction for quiet from Richard. I brought my eyes back inside and glanced at the floor at the foot of the open stairs. I quickly brought my hand up to keep myself from a loud exclamation of "Oh, my God."

My petite, all-black Curly was stretched out on the floor just to the side of the stairs. In her creeping predator stance, one paw extended, her knotted-up tail wiggling back and forth, she did not take her eyes off the cat door four feet in front of her. To her left, my calico was crouched down with a curved back and her best "worried about the world" look firmly in place above her white-and-flesh-colored bib. All four of her feet looked poised to run, but with Moe, I never knew whether the run would be toward the cause of worry or away from it.

Frances was sitting on the right side in her typical inspector position, up on haunches, front legs extended, and wearing that usual placid expression—a look that says, *Well, I'll wait to see what's happening before deciding what to do.*

Outside of this semicircle of guards protecting the door to their castle was Lucy. A couple more feet away, she was spread out on the fourth step of the stairs. Through the posts of the staircase, I could see her red heart tag and the white bib on her long-haired black body. Long white whiskers, indicating the bulk of an obese cat, were quivering while she waited to see what would transpire. She was gauging how long to wait and watch before fleeing the scene. There was never any question that she would leave any confrontation to the three more courageous members of our fur family.

As I watched these four cats protecting their domain from the foreigner wanting to take over their territory, I thought of all they had surmounted to arrive at this point of cooperation, working together for a common purpose. I then thought of Richard and me as well, as we went through the same process of amalgamating: transferring our households and bringing his two cats to join my two.

I had retired in 1999 from more than thirty-seven years of teaching. So, what to do? I was too burned out to sign up for subbing right away, although I did later do a few stints by request of a couple of coworkers. I am a project person—I need activity. I need to always be doing something. So, when I retired, I knew I had to find things to occupy my time and my interests. I had used up my remodeling interest and had done as much landscaping and clearing of land as I wanted to do, for the moment anyway. I wanted to go on to other things. But what would those other things be?

I signed up at Childhaven for a stint most of the day once a week with two-year-olds. It was the day of field trips, and I took part in visiting the mall, the pumpkin patch at Halloween, the zoo, down along Green River in the park, and various child parks. It was fun to hold little kids, read, play, and eat lunch with them. Then I would help put them down for a nap and sneak out to go home. I also signed up to do filing for the municipal court in Federal Way one afternoon a week. Then I took training for the diversion program of the Superior Court. This I kept up for seventeen years while the others fizzled to a close much sooner.

In 2001, I attended a creativity discussion group at a Barnes & Noble bookstore, where I met Richard. After twenty years on my own, I had not even thought about having another relationship. Three relationships with a shelf life of close to ten years each did not leave me with hopes for success in that department. I figured, *That opportunity had definitely been blown. No chance for that again. I'll be sitting on the porch swing by myself. And I'll be holding my own hand. Yup, I sure blew the chances for that together-in-old-age bit.* Then this relationship started. We joined our households and our cats as well.

Lucy, Frances, and Moe united in their concern about a possible outside threat.

As our animals learned to consider one another, collaborate, and resolve their conflicts, so did we, albeit painstakingly and through an abundance of trial and error. The process of learning to accept oneself and another, to speak up for needs and wants, and to give up regrets takes time and patience.

In January 2004, I attended a writing class at the senior center, and this gave me another answer for the rest of my life. One that required fewer supplies and equipment than my prior projects—no fabric, yarn, sewing machines, irons, or ironing boards; no paints, canvases, frames, papers, glues, pastels, pens, and inks; no hammers, nails, screwdrivers, lumber, saws, or measures; and no shovels, hoses, rakes, hoes, edgers, or lawn mowers. Not only was no room needed to store materials for this activity, but also no moving around was required. I certainly have enough ideas and experiences to draw upon for many years. So yes, I was ready to continue this stint of retirement.

40

SENIOR-STYLE MUSICAL CHAIRS

After Richard and I met in February 2001 at a Barnes & Noble bookstore creativity discussion group, in August, the group began meeting in my studio to make papier-mâché projects. We began seeing each other outside of the group in February of the following year, traveling from Burien to Federal Way and from Federal Way to Burien. In October 2004, we decided to "cohabitate," as Richard put it. An old school chum uses the term "undocumented spouse" for her live-in man. We began to check out retirement communities and condos.

With that plan, Richard had to give up much of his extensive shop and supply of wood gathered over many years. He had taught wood design at the Maryland Institute College of Art for sixteen years, besides creating and selling his own wood sculptures. He had spent fourteen years in the civil engineering department at the University of Washington as an instructional lab technician. In that capacity—according to him as a glorified janitor—he had been responsible for not only acquiring but also disposing of a multitude of materials.

From both lines of work and interests, he had accumulated a considerable amount of what he refers to as *dunnage*. This word, meaning the baggage or personal effects of a sailor, is also used for the loose materials or padding surrounding cargo to prevent damage. Richard's vast amount of wood and other materials of most any kind, size, or shape had filled a twelve by sixteen-foot shed, a built-on storage area, and some space in his two-car garage in Burien, along with his enviable wood shop machinery and tools.

I had lived in my same place since March of 1966. Although not always content, I had never thought of leaving, nor had I ever looked at other places to live. As Richard and I toured newly built homes in retirement communities, I became fired up over the thought of living with new materials, spacious floor plans, and open spaces. I became entranced with all the advantages possible. *But!* Those were indoor open spaces. How could I give up the space of my outer world to live scrunched up in such close proximity to others?

Always, there is a but! I would have to give up my house and two acres, extensively remodeled and landscaped over thirty-eight years. Albeit a wackadoo house—added-on, built-up, and unprofessionally finished by myself—but one I had made comfortable and enjoyable.

I was willing to give it up for Richard. But! Body and mood willing, I still like to work on my land, and more importantly, I love to look out in all directions to expanses of green and nature. And even more importantly, each spring I want to still eagerly await the chorus of frogs, the mating of ducks, and the arrival of new generations of fuzzy little ones in my pond! And allow freedom of movement for any pets I might have.

Slowly, we both came to the decision to amalgamate our households into my house and land. The three-month process of bringing his belongings from Burien to Federal Way was followed by a year-long process of settling in. And, of course, the never-ending challenge of learning to live together with more peace and harmony than disagreement and contention! Also, there was a task of answering ongoing questions: How do we work together when we are used to making all our decisions alone and taking every action on our own? How do we give up and give in when we both want our own way? How do we surmount our archaic, unresolved childhood issues? We both have plenty of those.

For me, how do I live with little privacy after total aloneness, and can I be gracious in giving up large portions of my space? Is it possible at this late age and belated stage to complete what we both lacked in the way of skills, our unfinished tasks of learning to be in a relationship?

Years ago, toward the end of a ten-year live-in relationship, I made the statement, "Oh Lord, that was another hormonal happening. I should have known better! Oh, why didn't I know better?" Well, I am so glad the hormones are still happening, and I am hoping that "Maybe, just possibly, this time I'll know better and learn more!" We would find out as we started the amalgamation.

Decisions abounded and the process of giving up, rearranging, and organizing began as Richard's loaded van arrived in almost daily treks

Juneau ignoring Richard's efforts to get a picture of her.

down the I-5 corridor from Burien. His office, which required space to accommodate his computers, printers, photography equipment, and multitudinous cabinets, tables, and desks, took over my twelve by twenty-foot garage turned into a bedroom suite. This sent one of my couches to Goodwill and an almost six-foot-long, buffet-like cabinet to the living room, which replaced a hide-a-bed couch that went to the back family room, displacing three old oak chairs. I had purchased these former Seattle Public Library chairs from Bargain World for $45, refinished and reupholstered them, and hooked them together to make a couch. I hated to part with them, but we tore them apart, adding oak dunnage to the new shed that Richard built to house his supply of wood from Burien.

We had already taken apart and dispensed with my waterbed, replacing it in the upstairs east bedroom with a bed given to us by my son. R's bed went into the west bedroom as a spare, and we sent two almost-new trundle beds, plus their bedding, to Okanogan for my daughter and grandchildren. My small television sets were moved around to allow his rather large single one to go into the back room for general usage. The TV I had used in the back room was moved into the small piano room closet behind sliding doors, as I now claimed that room for my own little hideaway escape. The small TV from my

And the moving went on...

bedroom moved to my desk in a little alcove, just outside R's new office. Yes, my office was what had been at the end of the garage years ago. After all, it is fun to talk back and forth with each other while working at desks and computers.

My washing machine and dryer moved to the deck to be taken by my daughter while R's double-decker ones moved into the tiny utility area. The living room was rearranged with his couch across from mine. My dining table went to Goodwill to make room for his larger expandable one. He won out—my other $45 oak chairs I had refinished and upholstered were moved out of the kitchen, with one going to Goodwill, one to the spare room upstairs, one to the crowded piano room, and one to the living room. Four deck chairs were given to my brother for his yearly reunions on his Lake Tapps property. Two chairs I acquired in Virginia nearly fifty years earlier I put up in our bedroom, while my bigger papasan chair went into the spare room, and I donated three other chairs to Bargain World. Ah, yes, definitely a game of musical chairs!

Were we the ones keeping Bargain World in business? Chairs, dressers, couches, multitudes of cushions, bedding, kitchen supplies, and clothes! Over the years, I had filled three large closets full of clothes, and I had to clear them down to one. And the stuff kept coming. What was that song? …*And the British kept a-comin'… on down the Missis-sippi to the Gulf of Mexico.* Only it wasn't the Brits who were moving down the road—it was the Hungarian. It was lucky for R that gas prices didn't soar until four months after he finished driving his loaded van daily. Of course, nothing was strapped to its rooftop, but I kept think-ing of the IKEA ad of the VW Bug with goods tied on top, reaching higher than the tunnel it was to go through.

For years I had heard people mention storage units, but I had room for extra things, merely recycling them into and out of the studio, or up or down the stairs. But, with the arrival of another household, the time came not only of having more things than space, but also of reaching a tolerance for discarding personal items. I rented a storage unit, which now houses an extra mattress of Richard's, a trundle bed, a bentwood rocking chair, an assortment of bedding and smaller items, and two seats from my daughter's car—removed so she could load other beds to take home with her. Some things just can't be parted with, like Nana Maud's kitchen table, used by us while my children were growing up and then by my son; it went into the storage unit, too.

At this writing, we still have leftovers sitting in odd configurations on the deck—two metal cabinets of Richard's, an old Wells Fargo trunk inherited from my uncle and covered with fabric, two trampolines sporting a dog bed, Richard's barbecue, and my washing machine that is waiting for my daughter to take. There is also a wonderful fir trestle table with its two benches purchased several years ago from Ernst. It had turned out to be too heavy and cumbersome for everyday use inside the house, but it was wonderful in the studio for groups doing crafts, eating meals, or just visiting.

All of these items are, of course, keeping company with the deck table, my four plastic deck chairs, Richard's four plastic deck chairs, two of his wood sculptures, and my wheelbarrow of herbs. Watching over it all is my two-foot-high, three-foot-long papier-mâché pig sculpture named Polka Porker. Maybe before the snow flies, the rest of the items will be distributed and the game of musical chairs completed.

41

Fur Kids' Trek South

*B*y far, the most fun part of the move was the inclusion of the Burien feline society to that of the one in Federal Way. At this point, I had my husky, Sitka, and two remaining cats, Curly and Moe. My animals have always been allowed free-range privileges, going out and coming in as they please. The cats eat out of the same bowl, always filled and placed a few steps up on the stairs to be out of reach of Sitka, who does not do stairs. Water comes from a communal pail just off the deck or from the pond about one hundred feet away. Of course, if necessity dictates, there is always the toilet.

Richard's two cats had never been outside and knew only one kind of dry cat food, served in individual food dishes twice a day. They had had little exposure to other people and none to other animals. Now, these disciplined, structured cats would be brought to my house to be combined with a very independent, topsy-turvy crew.

Richard brought Frances over on a Monday afternoon early in November. I called my vet to make an appointment, and the two of us set out with the kitty carrier in hand for a checkup plus rabies and distemper shots. The same veterinarian had been seeing my many pets for several years, including rescuing my huskies from their terrible accident. Even in that most trying time, I found him to show calming, matter-of-fact concern toward both pets and people, and I felt Richard would also be comfortable with him.

At the beginning of the exam, the vet exclaimed loudly, "Wow, I have never seen a cat of her age with such good teeth." Looking further, he repeated, "I can't believe she has such good teeth." As he continued the exam, he learned that she had not been to a vet since she was a baby and that she had spent her entire six-year life inside, with her only exposure to animals being the other cat she lived with. In discussing how extensive the shots should be, we told him we were combining our two households and Frances and Richard's other cat would be moving in with my two cats and a dog.

The vet's head went back. He pulled the corners of his mouth down, raised his eyebrows, and said, "Oh reeeeally." When Richard told him he also planned to let his cats become outdoor ones, he tipped his head back a second time, this time roaring with laughter, saying, "Well, I wish you well. And good luck."

It was fun to watch Frances in her new surroundings. At first, she was leery of everything and stayed in Richard's new office with his furniture from the old house, her own food and water containers, her litter box, and her scratchboard. In a couple of days, she was at the door examining the scene directly outside the office. Soon, she ventured forth a bit more but quickly did an about-face if I or one of my two cats approached. I was quite disappointed in the lack of manners and hospitality of my feline children—I had evidently done a very poor job of raising them. Either one, at the approach of Frances, would open her mouth wide, expose a full set of teeth, and hiss long and loudly. At which point, Frances would beat a hasty retreat back into the office.

I was quite familiar with Frances from my many visits to her house. She was curious about anything I put down, sniffing and exploring my purse and shoes on the floor. When my earrings became uncomfortable, I would take them out, but I soon learned not to put them on the coffee table. Everything was a toy to Frances—she would pounce on, bat at, or even abscond with anything left out. Coming in after a movie one night, I put my rings on the coffee table. One was a ring my son had given me, and it contained stones representing my two children and two grandchildren.

The next morning, the ring was gone. I looked under, behind, and around everything throughout the living room, dining area, kitchen, and hall. My ring was nowhere to be found. I was heartsick and didn't want my son to know I had lost his ring. Several weeks later, it returned beside a bookcase; Frances evidently had tired of the ring or of my sad face as I continued to poke under and around everything in sight each time I came to visit.

One day after the big move, Richard was sitting on the toilet reading a magazine with the door open. Frances, prone to following him around, wandered in, stopped by his leg for a pet, and then jumped into the tub. Spitter, sputter, and with a feline meowrring screech, Frances came sailing out of the tub, flew through the air, splattered water on Richard, hit the floor dripping, careened out the door, and disappeared around the corner. It happened to be the day the water department was turning off the water. We had, of course, filled the bathtub.

Richard's cats Lucy and Frances.

Frances did not take long to acclimate to her new surroundings. She was soon venturing outside to discover birds, squirrels, bunnies, and the five big dogs next door. Thankfully, I had fenced in the boundary by now. Frances is a curious cat and observes everything going on around her. Richard calls her The Inspector.

When he dug an eighty-foot ditch to add 220-volt wiring to the studio-turned-shop, and then again while two electricians were hooking it up, Frances was right in the middle of everything. Pacing back and forth, she intently watched each person perform his chore. The electricians periodically stopped their work to observe the observer observe them. Later, each mentioned his amusement at having each step of his work supervised by a cat. We thought she might be able to do the next hookup herself—if she hadn't been declawed, of course.

42

DOWN AND OUSTED

Ten days after the arrival of Frances, on November 11, we went through the same process with Lucy. She arrived in the carrier along with a scratchboard, food, water dishes, and a vanload of tools for the shop. We made the same trip to the vet, and again he exclaimed over the beautiful health and teeth of this seven-year-old cat. Once more he laughed at our hopes of not only combining all these animals but of changing the life habits of two of them so drastically. Little was I to know at that time that it would be changing the lifestyles of two people as well. But I'm getting ahead of myself.

Forgetting the vast individuality of all living things and thinking how easy it had been for Frances to take to the outdoors and all its delights, R made a big mistake. Less than a month after Lucy in the Skies arrived, he put her outside the door onto the deck. Up until then, she had stayed deep inside the office with her familiar things for some time and had just started to venture forth to other parts of the house. Now, she was ousted—forced into her first excursion outside, on December 7.

She crawled behind some things left out from the move and then immediately moved back to the sliding glass door to cry plaintively, long and loudly with a rhythmic opening and closing of her mouth. She was like a baby needing food or love, who once started keeps up the same crying motion until something interrupts him. Or until all hope is gone. I was not as familiar with Lucy as I was with Frances. When I had been at Richard's, she would usually stay in the back reaches of the house and far from me. Now I crouched down to observe her through the glass.

She is a black longhair with distinct coloring. On her front is a large white hourglass shape reaching all the way from under her chin down to her hip area. All four paws are very even and symmetrical, with each one ending in white in the shape of duck webbing. Her very wide, short, fat face is black with white whiskers and eyebrows that are the longest I have seen on a cat. Looking at her, I thought, "She's a Sylvester." Then her mouth opened wide in protest, showing her long, sharp teeth. I drew back, thinking, "Boy, I would not like to run afoul of that cat."

Lucy sitting on the toilet—but not doing her business on it.

Shortly, I gave in to pity at her wailing. As I took yet another Goodwill sack out to the deck, I opened the door so that, with belly almost to the ground, she could slink past me and into the house. With great stage behavior, she looked behind her to the right and then to the left, announcing to any who might see her that she was in dire straits of being attacked at any moment by deadly monsters in this strange new land. She slithered across the back room and into the now familiar office. Here she could sit in R's chair or climb up behind his computer.

Richard came in shortly and asked me why I had let her in. I replied, "She is not as adventurous as Frances. Left out, she might develop feline agoraphobia. I let her in."

On December 8, R put her out again and got busy moving and organizing. Much later in the day, he asked if I had let Lucy in. "No, I didn't." She didn't appear that day and didn't appear the next one. I kept going to the door where she had been put out—the same place she had cried to be let in. Still no Lucy! I wanted to go looking for her, but R said, "No, she will come back." He went about his business and didn't let on whether or not he was bothered by this. She was his cat—so of course, it was his call. The next day I went around the house looking at the crawl space openings. R said again, "She will come back."

I wouldn't have been so worried if it had been one of my cats. They had spent their lives outside as well as in. They had caught mice. They had been around the outer perimeters of the two acres, up to the road and down to the pond to drink. They had climbed over the dog pen fencing where I dumped leftovers for compost. They had been to the garden and could eat the squash left from the summer garden. But this poor little creature had never been out of the house before coming here and didn't even know what a leftover was. And she was not adventurous or brave like Frances. The next day R admitted he was worried about Lucy and was afraid she was gone.

On Sunday, we heard a faint meow and raised our eyebrows at each other. Afraid to hope, we first looked to see if it was Frances making the noise. Finding that wasn't the case, we went from room to room and discovered that the sound was loudest in R's office. I pointed him to the crawl space on that side of the house. He took a flashlight to check it out, came back for a crowbar, and returned shortly with Lucy in his arms. We were eager to hear about her five-day adventure, but this time she was very tight-lipped and would not share her story with us. We figured we all have stories we would rather not talk about and didn't push her.

The next day, R queried, "I wonder if anyone grooms cats?" I said I imagined that Sitka's grooming place would do cats as well and asked if he wanted me to find out. Thinking about it a bit, I asked why he wanted to know. He said, "Because Lucy smells so musty from being under the house." And then, with his own brand of humor, he added, "And, maybe it's time for her next traumatic experience." So, after her five-day crawl-space outing, Lucy went for another trek out in this cruel

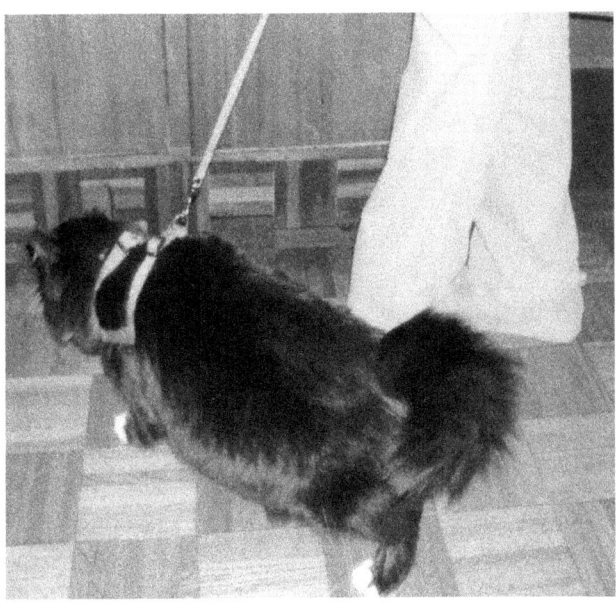

Lucy learning to like her leash training.

world of monsters to get a bath at the vet's. Now clean and sweet-smell-ing, she stayed in R's office for a couple of days before venturing out once again to slither around the house.

The day after Christmas, R once more put Lucy outside. Again, she went missing. A couple of days later, I was raking leaves in the front yard and heard her complaining. Right at the corner of the house, op-posite from last time and a short distance under the porch, there is a place in the foundation with an opening the size of a couple of bricks. Lucy was at the opening peering out with her big yellow eyes. She, of course, would not come out for me. I got a can of tuna and put it down outside the opening with the intention of coaxing her out. Hopefully, I could catch her and block her from going back in. She came out a bit for the tuna but beat a quick retreat before I could get her. Richard was more successful when he came home and brought her back into the house.

This time Lucy became more dedicated than before to her life as a recluse, refusing even to leave the office. One day, with a set to his jaw, R marched out the door to his van. He returned shortly with a blue woven harness. He put the harness on Lucy, pulled her out of his office into the house, and proceeded to walk around. Lucy refused to walk, pulling against the intrusion with her rear planted firmly on the floor.

R, extremely focused, continued without her cooperation to do what he had determined to do, which was to force her to walk in the harness. From sliding on the floor, she progressed to being half up and half down, then accomplished a sort of sidewinder manner like a snake. After several days of this treatment, a transformation slowly began to take place. From pulling against the harness or slinking along with her belly to the floor, she started to strut her stuff around the circle, head held high, and tail sashaying. She had gone from Lucy the slitherer to Lucy the swoosher in the course of a week. We could just see our drama queen waving her paw from side to side to the peasants as she paraded past. She would still hightail it back to the office if new subjects approached, but she had definitely started the transition into this amalgamated household.

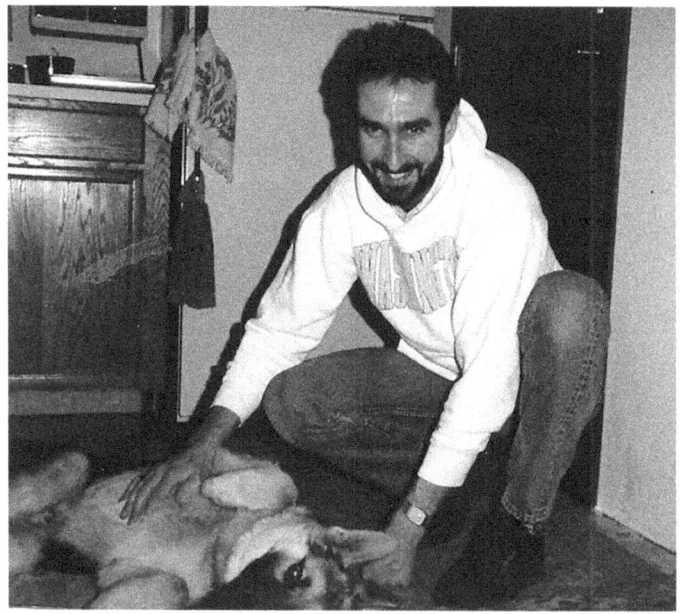

Grown-up son Chuck with his dog, Kona.

43

SILLY ADDS TEXTURE TO MY LIFE

"*P*ack your life with interesting experiences to make your life memorable!" proclaimed an article that encouraged continuing to add unique and different activities as a way to keep a memory alive. It stated that the same familiar activities tend to run together without your having a recollection of them, but a variety will provide a texture to the passage of time.

Well, Richard added texture to my life, and one of the ways was to add silliness. Absolutely, positively, nonsensical *silly*.

R says, "How wonderful of Seinfeld to give us permission to talk dumb. And about dumb. He gave us situations about nothing, the nonstory. They were nonconsequential sitcoms."

I added, "Yeah, the noncon sitcom."

Life with R has been an opening up for me. He is a sponge for soaking up knowledge and information in most any subject. Being with him is like a return to the delightful world of college days. Slowing down, getting still, and opening your mind makes so much possible. We have fun. Silly thoughts come up as we play with words, take an idea, and build on it, moving it here and then there, like abstract art. We might describe a thought, let it flow, and watch it develop to see how the other will respond to it. We might play with any ramification of an idea, lob it back and forth over a net of the ridiculous, and allow an evolution of stupid word plays as if we were back in junior high or probably more like fifth grade.

A present-time example of senior silly was when we were out to dinner and saw a man with tattoos covering his arm. I looked back and studied them. I turned to R and said, "You know, I don't object as much to those as I do with most tattoos. They are well designed, like South Seas or Pacific Rim art—overall designs that work well together instead of a mishmash of objects thrown together."

R replied, "We have overall good design, also. It's all age-related—it's called wrinkles."

Then again, we might revert at any time to a junior high level. Finishing the last two paragraphs of my final chapter, I sprang up spontaneously, danced around the back room, and sang, as I am often wont to do: "If I could sing like Bing, how happy I would be, ba ba ba boo, ba ba ba boo."

I heard from R's office, "Did you say something?"

"No, I was just exuberating."

R said, "Well then, exurber on. Just keep taking the librium."

To my "How's the day out there?" R will answer, "Well, there are no cadavers." I suppose that might be fifth-grade level.

When I reported that one of my optical floaters just ran across the street, R replied, "Well, one of mine just chased him. Life can be a farce."

When discussing the raised price of gas, I said, "I remember buying a loaf of bread for twelve cents from the bakery in Snoqualmie after church. Funny what any one person pulls out of their memory bank."

R replied, "If I were you, I'd leave it in there to gather interest."

Me: "Oh, you don't find interest in my statement?"

Our conversations touch all borders: the ludicrous, the ridiculous, the irreverent, and the downright gross, as well as sometimes more elevated ones. We touch all corners of the box—north, south, east, and west and sometimes right in the middle. I was once in Marlene's with R when my eye spotted Seventh Generation toilet paper. "OH NO—what an unfortunate name—recycled TP, right out of the outhouse, no doubt."

We both read in one of Patricia Cornwell's books about a very rare disease where a person is completely covered with hair, even to the eyelids. I mentioned how horrible that would be.

R said, "You know, it could come to that point."

"What do you mean?"

"Think of static added to the cat hair from our four cats." We envisioned cat hair flying up, attaching to us, and sticking out of our skin all over our bodies.

Finding a puddle one day, R asked, "Do you suppose there is a clunker-cat program?"

I replied, "You already know our cats are not purrrfect."

Richard and I doing what we love best—being silly.

One day I told R how, before he arrived on the scene, I left my bedroom window open at night for Curly to go out to catch mice, bring them in to eat on the floor by my bed, and leave their spleens on the floor.

R said, "You should have saved them. The health food stores might have wanted them."

I said, "No, they are poisonous."

"Well, you could use them as an end-of-life solution. You know, suicide by mouse spleen."

I countered, "Could be used on the *NCIS* program. I can see it now: 'What was the murder weapon? Why, mouse spleen, of course.' "

I have been known to be very slow on the uptake and temporarily misplace parts of my intelligence. One December, a couple of days into a thaw following a week with the pond frozen, its center was still solid while a foot or so around the edges was thawed. Three ducks were down at our end of the pond. I asked R if the edges were scum or ice, and R said it was ice. I asked, "How did the ducks get there?" R replied, "Maybe they swam under." I told him to watch and see how they would get out. A few minutes later, he poked his head through the door from the kitchen and said he had the official word—they had flown off. With exasperation, I said, "Well of course. It's not fair. They get to do all the fun stuff."

I have difficulty with change, and over and over I decry this modern world with all its complexity. One time when R thought I had griped too much, he said, "Yah, when those wheels first came out, it was simple— they just kept going around and around." He said the wheel was from China and came to Europe because of the lateral stuff but not the Americas because of geography, the mountains, and no domesticated animals.

I shot back, "Oh, did they invent the wheel because of domesticated animals?"

He talked about the materials being different; one culture made ceramic wheels but used them as a toy. I said, "How strange to think of the wheel being used as a toy but not put to a practical use."

He replied that the creative mind can go only so far at a time. And then he declared his family invented the wheel, but it just kept rolling down into the swamp, and after a few generations they gave up.

I said, "Mine invented the wheel too, and finally my grandfather thought of putting a hole in the middle."

"Oh well, my great-grandfather did several wheels, but he didn't get further than a square in the middle, but one time it was a triangle." He added, "I bet they discovered fire and invented the wheel on the same day; that night they burned the wheel."

On another occasion, I was looking in my *The New Yorker* humor anthology and read the sentence, "If the universe keeps expanding, what will it wear?"

My first thought was, "Well, what is in vogue at the moment?" Then I stopped to consider an all-important question—whenever fashion comes into play, what would the gender of the universe be?

When I read the sentence from *The New Yorker* to R, he laughed, continued with what he was on his way to doing, and then turned back with a grin and said, "I have an answer."

"Okay, what is it?"

"A quantum jumpsuit."

R is a minimalist—a conversational minimalist. I don't know if, as a child, he was discouraged from talking and is afraid of sharing too much, or if it is his way to confound others. Or if…

Today R came in and declared, "Higgs is revisiting the God Particle." God Particle? Usually when something out of my frame of knowledge is thrown at me out of the blue, it is accompanied by an expectation that I of course know about it. So, I ask a question to get a toehold.

Then I attempt to find out enough info about the subject at hand from the crumb of info thrown at me to see if I can answer with a relatively sensible response. This time I chose to own up to my ignorance and instead asked what he was talking about. R explained, "Higgs, looking into work proposed by Einstein on particle theory, called it the 'Goddamned particle theory' and that started the term 'the God Particle.'"

"Well, you know I am a literal person," I answered. "I didn't know if they found God's toe out in the desert somewhere."

During the time of a horrible winter, we watched a program on global changes. I said, "Well, it's certainly something else to be stressed about, along with the economy and state of unrest."

R said, "All of us retired folk can absorb the stress for those who are still working."

I replied, "Oh, good idea, and then they won't give off so much CO_2."

While watching a CNN documentary on running out of gas and the state of the world's oil supply, I thought about the young people today reacting to the dire state of the environment and the gloomy tales of what is coming for their tomorrow. I told R, "It would be so easy for them to feel justified to do whatever they want today. They could so easily have an attitude of 'Well, what does it matter anyway?'"

R said, "Well, let's go out and rob a bank."

I thought about the repercussions and said, "No, no, let's wait until we're, oh, maybe 87 years old. We'd have less time in jail."

We once thought about the saying that the one with the most toys at the end of life wins. I said, "Some people would think the sign of winning would be the most people at the funeral. Yours must be the one with the most learning wins."

He said, "No, I don't learn it all. It would be the one with the most exposure to learning."

Car trips often bring on the sillies. When we passed the Yahn & Son Funeral Home down in the valley, R said, "They should have reader boards for funeral homes."

"Yeah," I replied, "they could have previews for coming attractions. Could have 'And up next is the viewing of the lovely Jane Doe' or 'Poor John Doe has passed his time and is all done in now.'" Then, looking at the name of the funeral home again, I faked a yawn and said, "Ho hum, another funeral."

I once heard Barbara Walters say that her least-liked trait was not making up her mind. She said her gravestone could read, "On the other hand, maybe I should have lived." I feel like I spend my life sitting on a fence trying to decide which direction to jump. I told R that my inscription should be written on both sides of the tombstone. Or on the urn.

So often, there is something I don't understand at the moment, but later, after more reflection, I will get it. I told R, "On my deathbed, I will sit up, put a finger up in the air, and with an 'Ah,' say, 'I finally get it,' and drop back down onto the bed, saying, 'but it's too late now.'"

R: "Ah, Einstein was right."

Me: "Yeah, it's all relative."

44

FUR KIDS AMALGAMATION

*T*he transitional period for Richard's and my cats was one of fighting and marking territory. As I've mentioned before, because of several remodeling jobs, my house has a strange configuration. A central section can be circled clockwise through the living room, then the kitchen, the dining area, around the corner into the utility section, past open stairs, into a family room (called the back room—my son's former bedroom with the old back porch added in), then back around past the door to a bathroom on the right, and finally the piano room on the left (my daughter's former bedroom) to return to the living room.

This is a pathway often followed. In times of distress, when my neurotransmitters refuse to coordinate, I have wandered around this circle, hoping to restore my synapses. I have been known to stomp around it when my frustrated leftover three-year-old has had too much to deal with. It is also an organized pathway to follow searching room to room when something I had in my hand two seconds ago cannot be found. Richard and I sometimes find ourselves circling this route attempting to track each other down. And now, of course, the animals have found this circular horizontal racetrack ideal to chase one another or to lie in wait for an attack.

One morning, with the full complement of fur kids here, I went to the kitchen for a cup of coffee. Lucy was lying on the rug in the living room. Moe was curled up in her current nesting spot—a basket on top of a chest-high cabinet in the living room where she can survey people and animals passing through the living room from either direction. In more cantankerous times (maybe feline PMS), she can lie on the shelf beneath the cabinet and strike out at the ankles of those passing by.

I came around the corner past the bathroom door where Curly was standing. Frances walked from the kitchen toward me and, as she passed, Curly opened her mouth, showing a wide expanse of teeth while hissing contempt. Frances lowered her body to an almost Lucy-like slither, but bless her stalwart heart, she kept her head up and continued right on past my surly Curly. I had heard on the radio that you need to give attention to the bully, the aggressor, and not to the victim. So, I reached down and ruffled Curly's neck. At the same time, in a soft, loving voice, I declared, "Curly, you are being a rotten little snot!"

We started seeing Frances follow Moe around, trying to make friends, as if to see what to do in this great and different world she had been transported into. I could just hear the cat conversation. Like a second child, the newcomer Frances was saying, "Wait up! Pleeeze, let me come too. Why won't you play with me?" And Moe's response: "Oh jeez, leave me alone! Do you have to follow me all the time?!" I kept thinking of a TV commercial I'd seen: "Mottthhhher, Frances is touching me."

One day, R put Lucy outside and, turning around, told me that he was going to the shed to move more lumber. Moe was there doing her best to tell us, *I hope you are noticing that my nose is quite out of joint.* I let her out, also. Turning to R, I said, "Actually your cats are doing better with this move than mine. Maybe yours think they're tourists on a vacation and will get to go home any time now."

His reply was, "It's because my cats are the ones intruding upon yours." Oh, of course, I hadn't thought of it that way. It reminded me of when many foreign students were coming into our area. I taught art and would get all the non-English-speaking students. There were already several Russian students in one class when the counselor brought in three new ones. I took some time looking around the room, as I wanted all of them to be next to someone who spoke their own language while also sitting with English-speaking students.

A delightful young Russian lady, whose personality and artwork I adored, was sitting next to the door. She either misread my look of puzzlement as to where to put these new arrivals without reseating the whole class, or she was just very perceptive of the times and history. With a twinkle in her eye, she said, "Yeah, we've come to take you over." I think of her often.

Now I turned back to R and said, "Maybe your cats think they are here to conquer mine."

My cat Curly with Richard's cat Frances.

After dinner one night, R pulled me down on the couch with him. We sat and observed the animals. In her usual restless way, Moe was roaming back and forth along the back of the couch. Frances, ever the inspector, was sitting at the edge of the coffee table, doing her curiosity thing—surveying the scene. Lucy was hiding on the floor on the other side of the coffee table. Curly, my aloof one, was maintaining her neutrality in another room. And, of course, Sitka was right there with her head in my lap, demanding the attention she richly deserves. Once again, her expression implied, "Why won't you people understand I really am a lap dog? It is so unfair. I am on the floor when all these lesser creatures get up on the furniture and lounge around in laps." She added with a mutter, "Seventy pounds isn't that much."

After some conversation in front of the fire, R and I turned back to the animals. Frances had moved up to the top of the couch and was edging closer and closer to Moe. Each one sat staring at the other, neither of them giving in. Curly had joined us, and never one to slink or retreat, she had marched right up to Lucy near the coffee table. I thought of a Mexican standoff. Lucy looked like a bandito, whereas Curly could have met up with one because of that knot in her tail. However, Lucy was the one to beat a retreat, creeping along the floor. At the corner, she did a drama queen move, looking back to see if anyone noticed. Since no one coaxed her back into the room, Her Highness left the premises.

One night, sometime after the move, things were pretty much settled down. Curly and Moe were no longer snarling and hissing, Frances was no longer running sideways to get away from Curly or me, and Lucy was not slithering, belly to the floor, out of the way of anyone within her view. The temperature outside was below thirty degrees, and the curtains and blinds were all closed as Richard and I sat down to eat dinner at five o'clock. Suddenly two cats went hurtling by us into the living room, and a thump followed. I went to investigate. Frances was crouched on the arm of a couch, stalking Moe, who was hiding at the end of the couch behind a lamp stand. I went back to eat my dinner. After a few bites, I looked behind me to see Moe going clockwise around the center island, not quite running, but definitely at a faster pace than usual. Hot on her trail was Frances, following her step for step, around and around.

All was quiet for a bit as we continued to eat our meal. Then, hearing noises from the back room and worried about Moe and her ability to stand up to Frances, I again went to find out what was going on. I saw Moe standing underneath the staircase, looking out first to the right and then to the left. She was waiting for Frances to come back after her, eager for the next bout of fun and games. I returned to my meal and conversation.

That was the turning point of my relaxing about the animals— rather like the moment I had with my children's driving, when I could finally sit back and not watch every move they made. That is, the point of "Okay, you're doing just fine. Do it your way."

45

PLAY NICE NOW

*M*y fur friends were now learning to play with the new kids on the block. I have always taken care of my animals, and when they come to me, I give them some loving. When I lie down on the couch to read, there will usually be a cat on my chest and often one between my legs, and when I work in the yard, I will find two cats and a dog somewhere close by.

But I have never been in the practice of seeking out play with my animals. Through the Early Years, there were my children, neighbor children, and the run of the outdoors. Encouraging independence, I figure they have enough entertainment on the two acres I provide. Playmates abound in the squirrels, bunnies, moles, bugs, frogs, ducks, and visiting dogs. School kids and traffic can be watched on the road, and the neighbor's arrivals, exits, and yard play are all within viewing distance.

On the other hand, Richard has always had toys and play times for his cats. Now, all of a sudden, I find my cats are copying his and will roll around on the scratchboard or pounce on toys, sacks, or boxes thrown down on the floor. R has various batting implements, including a feather duster, and will play with the cats through the banisters of the open stairs. Besides the circular racetrack, they have this vertical playground. As we sit in the back room in our TV chairs enjoying *Boston Legal, House,* or *Numb3rs,* we can see and hear the cats chasing one another up and down. Or Frances might just sit up there and watch us. We may awaken during the night to thumps. Lucy is a heavyweight and can be heard plunking her way down the stairs.

Lucy had not only been ousted but she was also thwarted; Richard covered her food dish. Food presented a problem. I have always set food out for grazing at will and never had an overweight animal. Lucy, who was formerly fed on a strict regime, now had more food freedom

Richard's portrait of an alert Frances.

and was becoming obese. The first cat to show signs of stress from the move, she began losing fur along her legs. R took her to the vet for an antidepressant prescription, and the vet made the comment, "The perils of Lucy." I countered with, "Lucy's Laments."

When R restricted Lucy's eating, I moved my cat food supply to the two places I spend most of my sedentary time. I put dry food in the bottom drawer of my desk for when I work there or at my computer. Then I can just open the drawer and let my cats eat while I work. I removed the music books from the piano bench in the small room where I paint, mend, and do bookwork while watching TV and moved another cat dish of food into it. Then I just open the bench up when Curly or Moe want to come in and eat.

When a laser pointer was introduced, we discovered an interesting fact. My cats love to chase the little red dot when it is moved along the floor or up a wall. They jump and bat at the light, delighting in the activity and asking for more. R's cats, on the other hand, will not play with it. Neither one of them. They sit there with no reaction. We don't think they even see it. We wondered if those early years confined to the house caused this. Not much inside moves around, except one another. Maybe my cats saw, followed, and had so much fun with the laser because of their hunting outside.

One morning, R came downstairs and informed me that he and Frances do synchronized grooming. In the morning while R is shaving, Frances sits on the rug behind him, going through the gyrations of her morning bath. I don't think I considered the differences of cats much until R arrived on the scene and pointed out their individual characteristics. Curly is very independent, but she is also affectionate and often grooms one or the other of us as well as herself. The first time she started working on my arm, I was amazed at the coarseness of her tongue and also its strength.

One day, R said, "Curly is more taciturn than the others." I thought about that and then replied, "Yeah, she's from the Corfield side of my family." Curly never meows and howls only when she gets her knotted tail caught in something. There is a big difference between our cats in their vocalizing. All the cats I have ever had were very quiet ones. This may have to do with the way they were fed. There is little reason to howl when a constant supply of food is available. Moe doesn't meow but shows when she is displeased, becoming a constant motion machine, running back and forth underneath our feet. I believe Moe is from the more volatile Irish side. On the other hand, both of Richard's cats are very talkative, showing no hesitancy in letting us know they want something, sometimes in the middle of the night.

Frances has a huge tuft of belly fur, as if she had had several batches of kittens. One day I was standing in the passway just outside the kitchen where R was making a snack. I opened the door and Frances came striding in with a great sense of purpose. She looked left into the utility room, to the right at R, and then sashayed past the kitchen with her excess fur swishing from side to side. She continued until halfway into the living room, where, about-faced and with a high degree of feline intent, she strode back to the kitchen. There she stopped, moved her head first one way and then the other, and headed through the back room to the sanctity of R's office. I commented about the process I had just observed: "She is either a cat with a great sense of purpose who, like an absent-minded professor, has forgotten the purpose, or she is intent on giving the look of being so busy no one will give her more work to do."

R uses mousetraps to keep his cats off counters. I started using them for my white upholstered furniture; I did not want Lucy's long black hair there. A friend was over one day when I scooted Frances out of one of my white chairs and set a mousetrap on it. Andrea saw me do this and said, "I might sit there."

My reply: "Then you can take the mousetrap out."

Andrea's answer: "But what if I didn't see it?"

Having come from a family who constantly reminded us to look where you're going and watch your step, my response was, "Weren't you told to look where you sit?"

To which Andrea retorted, "Well, I've never had to look for a mousetrap before."

After a moment of reflection, I said, "You didn't spend forty years teaching junior high art or home economics, did you? I never, ever sit down without looking to see the condition of the chair."

I had thought the next big fun would be three months in the spring to see the reactions of the new cats to the outdoors. However, this time was sped up when the day after Christmas, R, standing at the door, said, "Shush, come here, be quiet." Frances was out in the driveway, scrunched down and pretending she was a big cat in the wilds hunting her dinner. Four feet away was a squirrel she was stalking. The squirrel disappeared up a tree, and Frances ran after it, screeching to a stop. She had never tried to climb a tree, but even more pertinent, she did not have the claws to do so. No longer able to pursue it, she turned around in disappointment and saw us watching her. Her expression mirrored that of a little kid caught in the act: "Oh no, Daddy saw me." Like a toddler first thinking when they fall down, "Did anyone see me?" instead of "Am I hurt?"

By spring they were all outside.

46

FELINE POTTY TRAINING

$\mathcal{S}$ince his cats used to stay indoors, Richard used litter boxes. My cats go outdoors except for the times I go on a trip. Cat habits, as well as those of people, are difficult to change, and my method of leaving a window open was no longer workable. R's cats would not start going outside to the bathroom and he continued to change the litter box for them.

During the process of attempting to train his cats, my cats became untrained. Why should they go out into the cold when these two intruders didn't have to? Mine started using the litter box also. R was forced into double duty since I refused to dump litter. After all, there is plenty of perfectly good dirt all around the house, reaching for two acres, which my cats not only know how to use but also did perfectly well before these litter boxes appeared.

We then started brainstorming kitty-door choices. We considered a segment to fit in the sliding glass door but quickly discarded that idea. Placement was a problem. Logistics dictated that the front and sides of the house would not be feasible; it needed to open onto the deck, which ran the length of the house on the north side. Two sliding glass doors, laundry facilities, outdoor plumbing, wiring, and my office area narrowed the choices. The asbestos siding, easy to chip or crack, was another problem to consider. We found a spot close to the sliding glass door, near the utility facilities with wood siding on the outside. R worked his saw-and-bolt magic to install the door.

More fun and games ensued. R moved the litter boxes from his office to beside the sliding door in preparation to take them outside once we had the kitty door in place. Back in Burien, R had had their litter box on an enclosed porch with a cat door, so this time R's cats were the resident experts, already experienced, and they immediately went in and out as expected, although not necessarily to use the vast outdoors as a toilet.

On the other hand, my cats had never encountered such an obstacle to their movement, and they didn't want to have anything to do with it. This process was going to be time-consuming, and we realized we had done well to start in the summer before cold weather set in. With the hole cut and the framework of the cat door in place but without my cats using it, R, attempted to induce them by taking off both translucent plastic covers and pushing my cats through.

Soon, all four cats were going in and out through the approved opening when R moved the litter box outside on the deck beside the door and put one of the flaps back in place. My cats quit going outside when they met this unfamiliar barrier. R's solution was to physically pick Moe up and put her through. Do you have a picture of Moe yet in your mind? Can you imagine her reaction? Richard said, "Whoops. One needs patience with animals as well as with women." I don't know if it is stubbornness, independence, or a bit of that old *I'll show you*, but in any case, that set her back a ways—and I perfectly understood. She was definitely MY cat.

It was time for creative problem-solving. What would be flippy and easy to go through, as well as transparent so Moe would not see it as an obstacle? For this sort of problem, I mentally brainstormed all the materials and supplies in every room in the house to find one suitable for the situation. In my office area, the light bulb lit up. Of course, the plastic sleeves to hold papers and photos in notebooks were transparent and flimsy enough to not seem like a barrier. I grabbed one, made it even less of an impediment by cutting it into vertical strips while leaving enough at the top to hold it together, and stapled it to the door top. The cats all used it. R didn't even need to push Moe through it again; she acquiesced on her own.

After a couple of weeks, I changed to a stiffer, less transparent sleeve and once again, all the cats freely used the door. Somewhere along this time, R disposed of the litter boxes or rather, stacked them up in the carport. As cooler weather approached, we began to attempt the real flap. We started with the outside, thinking they would put up with more discomfort to get inside for food, and then they would go out into the cold to relieve themselves.

Moe was again the great holdout. Before the new arrivals, I had never noticed her being so stubborn, but she became more so as time

Not the toilet training wanted.

passed. We picked her up and pushed her through. Once the real door was on, I propped it up with a chopstick so she could see the floor on the other side and know it was possible. Soon all four cats were going in and out with the real flap on the outside and the translucent plastic sleeve cut into strips on the inside.

We are all learning to settle in. Frances not only goes out a great deal of the time but also has chosen to stay out all night a few times. Lucy is going out now and even ventures off the deck and around to the front of the house before sashaying back to be let in. My cats go about their business as usual. Except I think Moe has an anxiety problem from the invasion and she is avoiding reality. I sometimes find her staring at a wall with her back to activity. Richard and I are also learning to consider each other, to curtail our irritation with not having everything our own way, and to attempt to speak with patience. Like the cats, it doesn't come easily.

One lazy Friday morning, enjoying the luxury of being retired, we went back to bed and, of course, were joined by Frances and Lucy. I told him, "I just realized that Moe and Curly never come to bed with us since your cats arrived. When I slept in my old bedroom downstairs, they would sleep on the bed with me. We started talking about my cats and his cats and their reactions to one another. We started "what-if-ing" a catfight. Of course, as happens with anyone—that is, to those in their seventies who still enjoy reverting to a fifth-grade mentality—we progressed to naming our teams the Burien Cat Team and the Auburn Cat Team. The As and the Bs.

We considered mascots. His team became the Red Woods, and then we visualized Frances with no claws trying to climb the tree and the flip-flopping and somersaulting that would result. Lucy, who at this time still refused to go outside, would, of course, not be up the tree or out on a limb no matter what its color or designation. If she did, she was too fat to get very far anyway. My choice for a mascot was, of course, a frog, and because my frogs are tree frogs, they would naturally be assaulting his tree team. My team gave a croaking cheer—rib-bit rib-bit—and we all jumped for the Auburn team. What came back at me was, "Who wood win? Who wood win? Red Wood, Red Wood!"

Our fifth-grade idiocy reining supreme! Yeah, reallllly dumb—but reallllly fun.

47

INTRUDERS FROM ALL DIRECTIONS

I am not necessarily a recluse, but I do like my privacy and hate to have it or my land invaded. The opossum was a case in point. A coyote periodically travels across the backwoods or up the side pasture, but I enjoy the reconnection with him—visually, that is. I did not like it when new neighbors along the northwest of my pond threw sticks into it for their three dogs. I went over and told them that when the pond dries up in summer, I mow it. I don't want to have to pick up a wood pile out there. They stopped.

A large intrusion occurred several years ago. Some people west of the pond kept their semitrucks parked at the back of their property that bordered the ditch leading into my pond. One day, I came home from school and, as usual, looked out the back windows to see how my world was doing. It didn't happen to be doing well at the moment. Several men in hip boots were in the pond wrestling a big tube of some strange material, pulling it toward them in waves. I called the people across the pond on the north, the ones who keep an eye on the goings-on around the neighborhood. They told me there had been oil dumped into the pond from the trucks and he had called the ecology people. The oil was cleaned up and those trucks were no longer on that property. Neighborly attitudes were not helped by this situation. Thankfully, I was only an observer.

As I mentioned before, the neighbors closest on the east side still have a pack of dogs who bark in a variety of decibels and trebles, intruding on my peace and quiet. For a while, R took the foghorn left from boating with Gran and Gramps and blew it to stop the racket at night. It would work for a little while, and then the boombox barking would start again. During the day, if I go into the carport to clean or get something, the dogs start their clamoring. If I attempt to garden on the east side of my property, the Doberman comes bounding down the bank to mark his territory with ferocious barking at the highest decibel

The neighbor's Saint Bernard passing through my land.

he can manage. The terriers are yippy-yappy little dogs, and I must admit I do not particularly care for those kinds of canines; the big one akin to a Saint Bernard has a very deep bass tone, which I do not find as objectionable. The neighbor most objectionable to me is the Doberman, who acts and sounds like he would really like to tear me apart.

There came a time when he attempted to do so. A few months ago, when I was starting a new critique group, I was waiting at the top of my driveway for a lady to pick me up. All of a sudden, three dogs surrounded me, bounding toward me in a loud chorus. Usually, the gate at the top of the neighbor's drive is closed, while the fences I had painstakingly put up keep intruders away. This time the gate was open, and the Doberman lunged at me. Thankfully, I had a notebook in my hands and held it up in front of me to thwart his attack. All that did was encourage him to attack me from the rear. The neighbor lady had appeared by that time, and she curtailed the assault by her pets. Her comment was "Are you mad at me? Don't be mad at me." I said I wasn't mad, just clawed.

After continuing to my meeting, I called Virginia Mason Medical Center. They had no openings but told me to go to the emergency ward, and I did. I had puncture wounds in both legs taken care of, and I went home with a prescription for heavy-duty antibiotics. By request of the doctor, I carried through with telephone tag to learn that, according to the neighbor lady, their dogs had had their shots. I am always up to date on tetanus. When I finally got home to change my clothes, I discovered that my jeans, although covered with blood, were not ripped. I was grateful to get the blood out, the jeans are as good as new, and the wounds would heal as well. I may, however, carry some bodily scars as well as the attitudinal ones I already have.

A month later, an ice storm knocked down one of my trees over into this neighbor's driveway. I thought I had better call someone to take care of the tree, but I realized I would not ask anyone to approach this property with all those dogs to contend with and a gate to go through. Later, the neighbor cut up the tree and he yelled down at me, "Now we're even." I responded with great exaggeration, "Well, I guess I wasn't going to wear shorts anymore anyway."

I remember a Mother's Day years ago with my whole family visiting on my deck when this neighbor and his two sons spent the afternoon roaring back and forth the full length of their land, about six hundred feet, on their motorcycles, disrupting the peace of our visit.

I guess the most spectacular intruder on my land was the time a few years ago when R and I turned off the TV at eleven o'clock and realized that two police cars, lights flashing, were sitting in our driveway. We watched as policemen with flashlights ran up and down the side pasture, stopping to shine their light up into trees as they went. We moved from window to window to watch them. Finally, when they came up close to the back deck, I opened the sliding glass door to ask what was happening. He said there was a robber in the neighborhood and to stay inside. Later, he came to the front door and, after warning me about leaving my car door unlocked, he said they had been chasing a young fellow who had been thrown out by his girlfriend's parents and was living in the woods. He had stolen from a house down the road and they had chased him to my street and over the hill into my south pasture.

That robber came to the same place where a few years ago, a newspaper delivery girl had dumped her extra papers onto my land. I went up to the road and confronted her about it. She said, "Oh, I didn't know that anyone owned that land." Duh. I told her every piece of land is owned by someone. You don't dump your garbage anywhere you want. I asked her how she would like it if I took my garbage and dumped it in her bedroom.

I thought back to the time before the arrival of the two new kids on the block and before the installation of the cat door. When I went away for a time, I'd leave open a small window above the washing machine and move the picnic table underneath it on the deck. With the screen down, my cats could go in and out at will. I put large containers of food and water inside for them, and in all but two summer months, they had water from the pond, or they could enjoy the change of flavor from the toilet. My son would stop in every few days to check on the state of feline felicity. I did this for years with no trouble.

No trouble, that is, until in 2002, when I spent two weeks in England to visit my English cousins. I didn't meet up with the Queen, darn it. But I did come home to find two wild cats had not only moved in and taken up residence but had also evicted my poor cats as well. These feral cats just took over, perhaps thinking what a fine bed-and-breakfast arrangement this was; when I walked in, they looked at me briefly and went about their business as if they owned the place and were now the ones entitled to this luxurious establishment. I thought differently, quickly cornered them both, and threw their sorry rears out the door.

Then I profusely apologized to my evicted darlings, who came back once the feral cats were gone. I was so glad my cats hadn't left to become wild themselves but had stayed close until I appeared to reestablish their proper domain. The frustration was short-lived and although the pride of Curly and Moe suffered damage, the house didn't; it could have turned out quite differently with any number of messes to clean up or require repair.

Now, here were Curly, Moe, Frances, and Lucy working together to protect their domain from intruders. Yeah, we are amalgamated.

48

TOO PAINFUL A DECISION

*n 2006, my grandson was to graduate from high school. Since he and his family lived on the other side of the state, I would need to kennel Sitka so I could attend his graduation. But the place I had taken my dogs before was full, and so was my vet. I called a vet in the neighboring town of Sumner, discovered they had a large establishment with an opening, and left Sitka there for the week while I took off to celebrate with my family.

Not too long after my return, Sitka was obviously not feeling well and not behaving as she usually did. She lost weight, wouldn't eat, was listless and lethargic, and would not get up to go out in the woods to relieve herself. I took her to my trusted vet of long standing. This was the same man who had taken care of her and Juneau after their accident. He said she was doing fine, just getting older like the rest of us. He extracted some teeth and sent us home.

Sitka kept getting worse. She lost more weight, lay around, and had accidents in the house. It was so painful to see this once proud and beautiful creature reduced to a sad state of losing ground every day. She was only eight years old, the equivalent of fifty-five human years. That is not old for a dog; Jude would have been eighty-nine in human years at her end. Old age also does not bring about this rapid a deterioration to such a debilitating state. I did not believe she had received a correct diagnosis, so I tried the establishment where she had been kenneled for a week during the summer; I wanted their opinion. After testing, they said she had *Giardia*, and they gave me medication and cans of prescription dog food. I went home with high hopes to faithfully follow the prescribed treatment of 500-mg tablets of metronidazole and to give special food to this very special dog of mine.

I had never heard of this *Giardia* thing, so I turned to the Internet. *Giardia* are tiny, one-celled, parasitic life forms found in contaminated water and feces, with the potential to cause serious illness. Inside a dog, giardiasis interferes with the overall digestion process, damaging the intestinal lining so it is difficult to absorb nutrients from food. If the dog is healthy, the trophozoites, the active stage of the parasite, may live in the lower digestive tract for years. If the dog has an immature or overburdened immune system, the trophozoites continue to multiply by dividing and can cause debilitating disease.

Several treatment options were listed, some with two- or three-day protocols, while others needed seven to ten days to complete the job. Flagyl (metronidazole), the one given to us, was said to be an old standby treatment for bacterial infestations causing diarrhea, and it is about 60 to 70 percent effective in curing giardiasis. The article went on to say it has potentially serious side effects in some animals, including vomiting, anorexia, liver toxicity, and some neurological symptoms, and it is not to be used in pregnant dogs. That did not sound good, but it might help that Sitka was definitely not pregnant.

She did not get better but did become thinner, could not hold her bowels, and would not even go outside to do so. It was so difficult to see her like this. She was obviously in pain and would just lie there looking at me with those sad, imploring, beautiful brown eyes. When my children were little, several times I thought, *I would rather be in pain myself than watch another who was.*

What do you do? There was nothing I could do except follow the regimen given to us and gather more information. Little is known about giardiasis, so it's hard to get definite guidelines for treatment, and different vets use different methods. I found out that several popular giardiasis treatments for dogs have not been approved by the United States Food and Drug Administration. It is also possible the available treatments only remove the cysts from the dog's feces without actually killing the *Giardia* living inside their intestines. More research is necessary before anyone can know for sure. Well, what chance do *we* have if *they* don't know?

We went back to the vet for another fecal smear and a bath and returned home with a different prescription—Drontal Plus (a combination of praziquantel, pyrantel pamoate, and febantel). But she still had no bowel control and no energy. We rigged up a line between the posts of the deck, allowing her to go a ways onto the land, and we eventually kept her outside. She was almost constantly relieving herself, losing more weight, and not eating. She kept going downhill with no results in any direction.

On December 16, 2006, I took her back to the Sumner vet for a last try at an opinion, and when I heard nothing encouraging, I requested him to put her to sleep. While I was waiting, I heard the gal who operated as a receptionist tell someone about their outbreak of *Giardia* last summer and added that they had a terrible time getting rid of it. I thought, *Oh God, I bet Sitka got it here and not out of the pond.* I did not say anything. I am a slow thinker, but as I drove home without Sitka, I became livid as all the ramifications gradually occurred to me. I was angry with this vet for not being honest with me, for not taking care of the problem in the first place, and especially for allowing Sitka to get it.

I could have dropped it there, but when I got home, I once more turned to the Internet and was glad I had. I read that in large kennels, mass treatment of all dogs is preferable, and the kennel and exercise areas should be thoroughly disinfected. Kennel runs should be steam-cleaned and left to dry for several days before dogs are reintroduced. Lysol, ammonia, and bleach are effective decontamination agents. I was then horrified to read that *Giardia* crosses species and can infect people. Our cats! I took the two dog beds to the dump and Cloroxed the deck on hands and knees with a scrub brush. All I could think of was our four cats getting it. And, of course, us. Looking back later, I wished I had taken Sitka to a third vet. But I didn't. It relieved me a small bit when I read the opinion regarding such cases varies from vet to vet. I was not quite as angry at both vets. I still was, just not quite as much.

Later, I said something to my own Edgewood vet, and he said dogs don't die of *Giardia*. Well then, why didn't *he* find what *was* wrong with her? Because they don't have constant diarrhea and become emaciated almost overnight with old age—not when they are only eight years old. That was what he had said—that she was okay, just old. I lost faith in both vets.

I felt so guilty about Sitka, on top of experiencing grief from her death. Anyone who has had a pet has made decisions regarding euthanasia. When a dog or a cat has lived eighteen years and their health is rapidly declining, what is the choice to be? Then again, what is the choice with an eight-year-old dog whose health is rapidly declining because of a parasite that is not responding to any treatment given? Would the choice be the same? And would the choice of the moment be tempered by the previous one, two dogs back, who I should have put to sleep earlier? At that time, I didn't think I had the right, and because of that, Jude spent time in pain.

When Sitka could no longer manage her independence, I think she gave up her oomph for life. She didn't really leave the property for the road, but before she was sick, she loved to roam our two acres, and she did go back to visit the neighbors across the pond from us. I asked them if Sitka was any nuisance to them and they said no, not at all.

Sitka was the last dog for me. I will not have a dog penned in and restricted. I am too kinesthetic to tolerate confinement. I loved to watch Sitka fly through the air when she saw mole movement in the dirt, or stalk a coyote who was trying to avoid detection by sneaking through the backwoods. It is painful to see any animal not having freedom of movement. Large dogs like Sitka should be east of the mountains with acres to roam free. I often burst out with the song lyrics from my childhood, "Don't Fence Me In."

My granddaughter Shannah cuddling with Sitka.

My backyard—outdoor space that pets need.

And I will not go through such decisions again—it is too painful and causes too much guilt. So much guilt in life! I miss her, and I wish she were back here sitting on the floor next to me while I read, with her paw on top of my hand like she used to. I would reach down to pet her, and she'd put her paw on top of my hand. I'd pull it out to reach down again and she would move her paw and put it on top of my hand again. She wanted to hold hands. Maybe it was an alpha gesture, and maybe she wanted to have the upper paw. Well, she was the top dog in my book.

49

LINES TO DRAW

I have no say over most things in the world, but in my own world, on my land, I can draw some of the lines. How far does my responsibility go? Where? How? Why? For whom? When? Can you undraw a line? Is there a better one? What is my fit in this universe?

Who decides? Choices always need to be made; questions always accompany them. While killing mice and moles, swatting flies, or chopping slugs in half, I believed my actions were okay. When I was criticized for hitting an opossum over the head with a two-by-four, I started to question my actions. I needed chemical sprays to diminish the yellow jacket population so I could live here also. I began to extend my thoughts to the actions of others as well. And I questioned where the lines are drawn in that proverbial, rhetorical sand.

Just where do you Draw the Line? We seem to have become a nation obsessed with looks rather than character. I read an article that implored us to learn to tolerate less perfection for our world to survive. How clean is clean? How manicured do we and our yards need to be? We seem to be obsessed with cleanliness. Clean is good up to a point, but it can become compulsive. The overuse of soaps and cleaners has far-reaching effects on our land and the quality of our water. I know a woman who uses three clean towels with every bath—one to stand on, one to dry with, and one for her hair. Literally tons of soap go down the drain and out into our waterways every year. I know people who use antiseptic on everything, even with the scientific findings now of the physical disadvantages to our bodies. I feel nauseated just walking down the cleaner aisle of the grocery store from the strong smells.

I must admit, as I drive around, to raising my nose and feeling superior when I see those manicured, perfect yards so many people take pride in. It almost makes me ill to drive in nearby Kent Valley, where wonderful, productive farmland has been covered over with pavement

and industry, and that practice is fast creeping further south through the Auburn, Sumner, and Puyallup valleys. Of course, I have no say on the matter, either on land use or the chemicals used around me.

But I do have the say in my own little world, and sometimes I don't know which way to go. At seventy-five years of age and after forty-six years on my two-acre corner of the universe, I get tired of all the down-on-my-knees work of keeping things up by hand. How long will I be able to maintain my land myself? All the years of clearing, landscaping, and loving upkeep! I get exhausted, and every few years, I have someone come and spray the weeds on the driveway, and then I buy some products to make life easier.

Then I let those things sit in the shed because I don't want dogs, cats, grandkids, great-grandkids, and me walking through chemicals on the grass. I want to keep my pond safe for frogs, ducks, and fur kids when they drink from it. I don't want chemicals sliding into the ditch that empties into the pond and from there into Lake Killarney. I don't want to put those "wonders of manufacturing" into the Puget Sound and the Pacific Ocean. I think to myself, *How lucky I am to live in this corner of the world with lakes, the Puget Sound, and the ocean. I want them protected so they will continue.*

But I have found that without the use of some of these objectionable substances, I could not hire people to clean my gutters or keep my woods free of dead trees and branches. So, I have resorted to chemicals to lower the yellow jacket populations so that my gutter and wood-chipper men can do their work. After all, I would not let termites demolish my house! The question always comes back to where to draw the line.

I have thought back to the hours of weeding I've done by hand in my nearly fifty years of living here. When I put the second story on the house, one of the septic system designers delighted in scaring me with tales of a wetlands declaration. The lady next door to my son was restricted from selling her house because her land had that designation. Knowing that buttercups thrive in waterlogged land, I proceeded to rid my land of them by hand before the inspector came to hopefully approve the septic system. The resulting trauma to my body brought about a five-year-long condition called polymyalgia rheumatica. Since then, I just try to keep the buttercups out of the gardens, not the pasture, but I still do it by hand.

Yes, how to Draw the Line? Does the method used to accomplish what you want make a difference? Flyswatters, bug sprays, or two-byfours? Decapitate the dandelion or spray it? Going back to that article encouraging people to tolerate less perfection, it advocated reducing pesticide dependency, practicing cultural rather than chemical therapy on turf, and choosing the least toxic product for any job. We use pesticides and herbicides to kill pests and weeds, which leads to the destruction of our land, water supplies, and environment. People seem to think nothing of calling in exterminators to rid their homes of rodents and insects and even just to prevent them. Homeowners and businesses give priority to presentation in the form of manicured lawns and golf courses free of any unwanted weeds, businesses with weed-free areas of bark and rocks, and parks and play areas in pristine condition that show evidence of the use of toxic chemicals. Who is affected? Millions who are drinking water contaminated by chemical runoffs definitely are, and even those walking through the area.

Why Draw a Line? Many are so determined to keep regulations and controls out of their lives that they are willing to jeopardize the future of their (and our) larger world. Lately, we have seen what happens to our economy and our environment when regulations are taken away, leaving it free for those who step in and do what they want for personal gain. It's so easy to avoid inconveniences, take what we desire now, and ignore the dangers of what may come about in the future, even though it will be disastrous for children and grandchildren. There are those who insist, "Oh, pooh, that's not going to happen. There is no global change." I say they are gambling with the lives of future generations. I care more about my grandchildren than that. I care more about your grandchildren than that, also.

Draw the Line for whom? Making choices from a narrow stance of what I want, how I look, and what I can get for me is very different from those made for the greater good of all, now and for future generations. Emphasis on the greatest good for the most people with the least intrusion on the health of all animals, plants, water, land, and atmosphere makes the most sense to me. I know what an ultimate good for all is not. It is not choosing for your own momentary or monetary wants instead of for the health of people, nature, and the environment. I wonder if downplaying the probability of "it affecting me" is the reason people perpetrate so many unhealthy practices. I see those who minimalize the harm from exhaust, industrial wastes, insecticides, cleaning agents, pesticides, and synthetic fertilizers on our environment; who dismiss the effects of artificial colors, preservatives, additives, and hormones used in our food supply on our bodies and brains; and who ignore the consequences of chemicals we apply on our skin and hair in the pursuit of so-called beauty. Living in Virginia, I saw people ignore hurricane warnings—maybe if you are often threatened by warnings of possible damage, you get used to them and ignore them.

I remember a conversation several years ago in the teacher faculty room about Agent Orange and so many other things accepted at the time that were detrimental to our health but accepted, nonetheless. The librarian's comment was, "Well! We'll all be in it together." My thought at the time was *What avoidance!*

There must be a better line. And why are we not drawing it? A decade ago, I started asking questions about my choices—and here I am asking more. I finally gave in and bought hornet spray so I could get my gutters cleaned. I recently learned there is a hornet man who vacuums out yellow-jacket nests and sells them for research. Bless his heart. I wish I had known about him before. My questioning increases as global climate changes become more and more apparent. With some of the worst natural disasters in history happening, why is our country and our world not more concerned about the ultimate good? Where is the morality of those inflicting such drastic changes to the world we live in? Why is self-interest more important?

When to Draw the Line? Before it is too late, I hope. However, with the increase in natural disasters and global changes all around us, it may already be too late. A newspaper article reported that acre for acre, American homeowners apply more pesticides to their yards and homes than farmers do to their fields. But, on the other hand, my daughter, by necessity, drives to her teaching job through apple orchards, breathing in that horrible spray day after day.

Bug bombs, ant traps, flea products, mothballs, fly strips, wood preservatives, disinfectants, weed killers, houseplant sprays, and garden insecticides are used by seventy-five million households. An article from *Garden Talk from Sound Values*, published by *The Seattle Times*, stated that a 1991 government study found traces of herbicides in rainwater in twenty-three states, and drinking water in thirty-eight states contained detectable amounts of seventy-four different pesticides. Not to mention the pesticide residues consumed each day on fruits and vegetables.

Of course, add to the list the chemicals and colorings from sprays, curling and straightening aids, makeup, tattoos, deodorants, cleansers, perfumes, and fingernail applications and removals on the semipermeable membranes of the body.

I am sure there would be even more chemicals now. Remember: Tolerate a little less perfection, immediately reduce pesticide dependency, practice cultural rather than chemical therapy on turf, and choose the least toxic product for any job. Think vinegar!!!!

Can you Undraw a Line? Is it possible to repair what has already been done? Can the destruction of our land be turned around?

In any relationship, there are differences of opinions and ways of looking at any issue. And with animals, people, the environment, and relationships, where do you draw the line and who gets to say where that line will be drawn? There are always questions.

50

STILL MORE MILES

*T*he twenty-first century, the third millennium, and my Later Years have arrived, showing evidence of wear, tear, and passage of time, plus a sense of more shifts and changes.

So much has been going on: media explosion, globalization, increased interaction with others, growth of digital media and the Internet, increased expression of ideas, introduction to other cultures and backgrounds, selling and buying online, and the ability to immediately research and learn about anything. I can experience the whole world without having to leave home—ah, my kind of happening. Along came the e-reader, Wi-Fi, and the iPod. R and I, along with four cats and a dog, have watched *Keeping Up Appearances, Grey's Anatomy, House, Numb3rs,* and best of all—*Boston Legal.*

It was a time of turbulence and horror as we experienced 9/11, wars *on* terror, and wars *of* terror around the world, accompanied by an increase of violence in games, shows, and literature. Along with advances in technology and robotics, we saw evidence of the energy crisis and alarming changes in climate and environment, followed by the global financial crisis of 2008.

It was a time of some of the worst natural disasters in history, with extreme destruction from cyclones, typhoons, hurricanes, and earthquakes: In 2003, one of the worst heat waves in history in Europe killed thousands. In 2004, a magnitude-9.3 earthquake off the west coast of Sumatra was the strongest earthquake in forty years, resulting in a tsunami with a death toll of approximately 230,000. In 2005, a Kashmir earthquake killed 80,000, while in the US, Hurricane Katrina was followed by Hurricane Rita. In 2008, a magnitude-7.9 China quake killed 69,000, and Ike, the ninth most destructive hurricane to ever make landfall in the US, hit Texas, Mississippi, and Louisiana. Then, on March 11, 2011, a magnitude-9.0 Japanese earthquake touched off a nearly-hundred-foot tsunami with thousands of aftershocks, many with a magnitude of 6.0 or more.

While movements were taking place in the earth's plates, the economy, technology, and the moral integrity of our business and government leaders, changes were happening in my little world also. More aware that disaster can hit at any time, I began to shift my gears and way of thinking. I realized my idealist world would not go on forever; nor would my life. At so many times through the years, I have automatically assumed the situation of the moment would continue, even to the point of thinking the sunny weather today would, of course, be there tomorrow. I have thought the agony at the time was to be with me for the rest of my life, or conversely, the ecstasy I was embroiled in would be there forever. How silly, after eight decades, to be amazed in the fall when the rains return.

All the stages I go through contain a mixture: good times between bad ones—or maybe it's bad times between good ones. Recently, I breathed a deep sigh of appreciation that all my close people are in a good stage right now. *Wow, all at the same time!* I savored this contentment and vowed to be mindful of great enjoyment until the next stretch of pain, disappointment, illness, or death plops down in the middle of my world. Another lesson to learn: Never expect any point of time to last. I vowed to not only savor what is here while it is here, but to enjoy it deeply.

Through these later years, I have watched my children go through many of the same pains and disappointments I experienced in my own life, and I recognized even sooner some of the same mistakes my grandchildren were making. Poor choices narrow future choices, are often not reversible, and can lead to deep heartache when the inevitable consequences arrive. Our actions and behavior, if not brought up to a level of awareness, can bring about defensive behavior when the very people we care for the most are bringing them to our attention.

Oh, defensiveness. That habit of immediately fighting against a behavior brought to our attention by another. Especially when we aren't able to stop, hear, think, decide if it applies to us, and be willing to admit it, much less take the necessary steps to make any changes to bring about more productive and satisfying results.

I wonder if my children and grandchildren realize the mistakes of poor judgment I made; or maybe not because I had been no more ready to admit my failings than they are. At one time, I remember thinking, *I am learning in my seventies what my daughter is learning in her fifties, and maybe, oh maybe, her daughter will learn in her thirties.* Oh, what a blessing it would be if my twin great-granddaughters would learn in their teenage years (the best time) all those missed lessons—as R would call "the missing dots." And that all-important missing dot—to learn that the only way to change what is happening to you is through your own insight into your own thoughts, decisions, and actions. And that you are the only one who can bring about the necessary changes.

I wish I had learned earlier the skill of thinking ahead to consequences, of making choices for what I want to happen tomorrow, and the next year, and the next decade. I didn't. I seemed to go like the animals—day by day. Actually, the animals parading through my life during the Middle Years triggered my questioning and my reevaluation of choices, and here in the Later Years, they have helped me shift my gears to learn new ways.

Richard and I watched the cats as they adjusted to living together; the cats watched us as we did the same. I wish WD-40 would work on lubricating human and feline brains to bring about a speedier and vastly needed shifting of those gears, but slowly and surely the gears did move in a better direction. R and his cats, Frances and Lucy, gave up their cozy home and structured living to accept moving in with all these strange new creatures with a very different and topsy-turvy life. Curly, Moe, and I were in this boat together, with our space taken over. Sometimes I felt I had given up too much—studio, bedroom suite, my closet, and even the side of the bed I had slept on for forty-seven years.

Our cats are all female, but it occurred to me that some of the same types of characteristics of gender differences might apply: Does Curly hiss in an attempt to shut up a sister? Is her distance and lack of mingling reminiscent of a male attitude? We don't know if the dance between Moe and Frances is a bid for a relationship or an attempt to threaten and intimidate. Moe turns her back to us and her face to the wall, choosing minimalist communication. Lucy picks up her marbles, runs away from what she doesn't like, chooses to be afraid of some things, and sticks her nose up at others she regards as beneath her queenly dignity, correctness, or intellectual level. I suppose my tendency to observe and comment on what I see going on would be commensurate with Frances, who has been called The Inspector. There is a difference between observing for a learning purpose and for indicating to one another that they haven't howled, purred, or hissed with the correct choice of meaning, inflection, tone, or volume. We both have to watch ourselves on these attitudes and behaviors.

I learned late in life that to get better results, it is necessary to revise thinking as well as actions. I was determined to make my relationship with Richard work. We both had issues from our pasts that we brought with us into the present, but this time I wanted to learn the lessons I had missed earlier in life. We found that hurt feelings and defensive attitudes get in the way of regard for each other. With agony and backsliding, we are working through focusing on issues instead of defending ourselves, trying to be right, blaming the other, or refusing to relate. We are learning the other person's behavior belongs to them and has nothing to do with us. The question seems to be: Do we care more for our archaic defenses or our relationship?

What are our priorities, what are we willing to give up, and when are we willing to give in? Life seems to be full of that. And, like all of life, sometimes it seems like the loss of too much territory; sometimes I feel hissed at once too often; and once in a while, I need to blow. Maybe I should have done like the cats and peed on the furniture. No, I would have had to take care of it. Blowing off steam occasionally is better. I just need to be allowed to do that, and I need to allow R his impatience, irritation, and directiveness.

Like with the land and environment, we are working to keep toxins out of our relationship, to tolerate a lot less perfection, to tune into the lesson that life really isn't fair, and to accept it is not a game for equaling out scores. Yes, more acceptance of another person involves a different way of being and thinking; it involves conflict resolution, patience, cooperation, and equal responsibility, taking the risk to honestly share with another person, and it does no good to expect others to be what we want. They won't do it, so why expect it?

We find it hard to change, but we keep at it. Yes, we have more miles to go in Relationships 101. To hiss or to purr? It is very seldom purrfect, but most of the time, it is getting better as we learn more lessons together.

You hear the expression *Location, location, location.* I am so glad this is the part of the world I happened to drop onto, and this little corner is the one I chose for my own. It was a wonderful environment for children and animals. It is a wonderful environment for me. I hope it stays healthy for a good long time to come.

I believe timing, timing, timing, and the moment in history are equally important. When my mother-in-law and I were talking about the modern advances and advantages of today but were also a bit leery and fearful of the possible directions in the future, she said, "I have lived in the best of all possible times." I agree with her and feel I have also been blessed along those lines.

What comes next? At this stage in life, as at the beginning, I still never know how it will turn out. I just have to go day by day and accept what comes. I thought of an old saying: *I did the best with what I had for where I was.* Actually, I did pretty well. I ended up with two wonderful children, two lovable grandchildren, five great-grandchildren, and even a very good man to hold hands with in my old age. Okay, so … what is next?

The pond dries up in the summer, and I mow it, leaving a large flat area. For years I have thought, *I could mow a big circle shorter than the rest, sink a hole, and use it as a putting green.* I did keep those putters. Yeah, maybe this summer.

EPILOGUE

I look at the fir branches tossing in the wind while a couple of squirrels play tag on the trunk. The clouds chase one another around in the sky, and ripples lap at the edge of the pond. I step outside on the deck to see if that special feeling is in the air yet, the one that speaks of a change of season. Flinging my arms out, I say to myself, *I think I feel spring in the air.* Closing my eyes, I inhale deeply from my toes and let my breath explode back into the air. *Oh, how I love the change of seasons. I can smell it. The air is so vibrant, like it's singing a song of life.*

I look around at the furs and feathers within my vision—Curly at my feet, Lucy on the picnic table, and ducks in the pond. Growing sad, I think of the latest fur kid I buried, my part wolf-husky. Looking inward, I imagine Sitka settling deep into the soil, fertilizing this land she loved. *I can just see her spirit sitting on a cloud, with her proud head lifted high, still howling at every full moon.* I reflect on my own life and think, *I am learning so much.*

At the pond, I see a duck head go down and a tail go up, and I think, *That mallard is telling me to accept what is here right now.* As his tail goes back down and his head pops up, I add, *And, let it go when that moment is gone.*

Changing pace, I look down and count seven molehills. I think, *The ground is molting.* Feeling mellow, I say, *Oh, all right, I guess I can coexist with the moles. I'll honor their nature, too.* Scrunching my nose and mouth in disgust and shaking my head, I raise my shoulders to add, *I doubt I'll ever be easygoing enough to honor the nature of slugs. Oh, well, you do the best you can.*

Turning to go inside the house, I notice all across the eaves of the deck tiny sacs holding dozens of wiggly baby spiders. I remember last year they all broke open on the same day with freshly hatched spiders on dozens of single threads bursting forth from each sac. Those dozens of webs holding wiggly babies hung down across the back of the house like colorful beaded curtains. These young spiders were ready to grow up and spin hundreds more beautiful webs, each one waiting to collect early morning dew. Each one, like all of nature, with its own special beauty; each one a work of art. *Right here on my deck posts, I have my private spider-art gallery.* After a pause, I add, *And catch lots of summer flies.*

I settle on a principle: *Honor with dignity all of life.* Then I add, *Make the most thoughtful choices possible, learn the lesson to be had from every mistake made, and then let go and move on.* I chuckle, thinking those principles give me permission to be free of my guilt and anger. I decide that, as one season is fully there before it changes and gives way to the next, I can fully enjoy each thing in its time while it is passing through my life. Continuing with that thought, I add, *And then I can let it go.*

Still thinking of the changes in nature, the uniqueness of all life, and how very special we all are, I whisper, *Right now, thousands of pollywogs are pushing out their frog legs, ready to join friends and relatives in their springtime chorus.* Shaking my head with wonder and with a smile traveling down to my toes, I think, *We all change in our own ways, but we all change.*

Just then, I hear the noise I wait for all year long. Frogs in the pond start singing their hearts out. I stick my head inside the door and yell, "Richard, the frogs are awake!"

Looking back at the pond, I think, *Yep, all's right with the world.*

Acknowledgments

I'd like to express great appreciation to all the writing groups who have encouraged my writing and applauded my stories. I would like to give special thanks to Mi Ae Lipe of What Now Design, for the extensive, time-consuming, and caring editing she has performed.

My Grandma Corfield said, "You do what you gotta do, child!" My addition is, "Persevere, my dear! And in any situation, there is a lesson to be learned. Find the learning!"

I would like to express belated thanks to my folks for the care and love of my children while I finished college and for their acceptance of my traipsing across the country. And much gratitude to my beloved in-laws for acceptance and love of me and my children and for opening possibilities of expression to feelings and opinions, to letting loose with following our own selves, and, of course, for the exposure to horses.

I have been blessed with wonderful Grands—Shannah and Josha—as well as Greats—Hayden, twins Madison and Alyssa, and twins Joseph and Jackson.

My words to my children are "How very proud I am of you—of who you are; what you have always been; the good, caring, and responsible people you are; what you have accomplished; and what you have meant to me. You are more than I could have ever hoped for, have brightened my life, and given me joy. As always, I love you bunches."

Chuck has since left this earth but will always remain "the Hero in My Life." Laurie has become my best friend and remains the heroine in my life. Richard for twenty years added intelligence, love, warmth, and silliness, as well as his cats. Bless you all.

About the Author

Raised above Snoqualmie Falls in a wonderful world of nature, Dianne Corfield Searle Macdonald would forever tune into nature and animals while raising two children and teaching art and home economics for nearly forty years. She proofread at the Institute of Early American History and Culture, published articles in home economics and art magazines, had a fun run of Individual Learning Activity Packages (LAPs), and illustrated a book for a dear friend. After retirement, she took to writing and has published several times in a quarterly writer's magazine.

www.ingramcontent.com/pod-product-compliance
Lightning Source LLC
Chambersburg PA
CBHW051302120626
46547CB00015B/2060